That Was Really Something

Books by Howard Nelson

Poetry

Creatures (1983)

Singing into the Belly (1986)

Gorilla Blessing (1990)

Bone Music (1997)

The Nap by the Waterfall (2009)

All the Earthly Lovers (2014)

Others

Robert Bly: An Introduction to the Poetry (1983)

The Wages of Dying Is Love: On the Poetry of Galway Kinnell (1987)

Earth, My Likeness: Nature Poetry of Walt Whitman (2010)

That Was Really Something

Howard Nelson

2018

Library of Congress Control Number: 2018955731

ISBN: 978-0-9976766-9-3

Printed in the United States

Published by

Groundhog Poetry Press LLC

6915 Ardmore Drive

Roanoke, Virginia 24019-4403

www.groundhogpoetrypress.com

The groundhog logo is the registered trademark ™ of Groundhog

Poetry Press LLC.

Contents

CAMPING ALONE

My friend Antler spends weeks alone in the wilderness every fall.

I have never spent any time camping alone, maybe two or three nights —

once when I got lost

and after wandering around the woods for two hours in the dark

I just lay down and slept in the leaves.

Antler talks about having to get used to walking on two legs again

when he returns.

He says that every year he leaves a little more of himself in the woods,

and that someday there will be more of him out there than here.

I think it may already have happened.

Someday, maybe, I'll go to some lonely spot and pitch my tent

and spend my days doing what one does when alone in the woods

and sleep night after night under the ten thousand stars.

But not in winter. Another guy disappeared in the Adirondacks last week —

it happens every year or two.

They found him, but not before

he froze to death.

Solitary heart attack while temperature, snow, and night were falling.

COYOTES

The dogs of the woods have come back

from wherever they were. I don't see them often,

for they are too secretive, too canny,

but I do see one now and then

trotting across a field on some solitary mission.

Often I see a scat with hair woven in in the middle of the path.

And I hear them singing, yipping and howling,

solo or in chorus, somewhere in the neighboring dark.

People are alarmed. They're livestock killers—

though there are very few sheep around here,

and the calves are in little crates,

or in the big barns, never out in the field.

I lost a cat—a young male who liked to go into the woods.

Then he just disappeared.

It could have been coyotes that got him.

Hunters are rising to the occasion.

One method with coyotes is to use dogs—

to fit them out with radio collars.

The dogs do the searching and tracking,

while the men sit in the truck,

and when the coyote is pinned down,

the men come and finish the job.

Coyotes rely on their ears to avoid danger.

They can detect hunters that are a mile away.

Coyotes have a special tactic

to avoid predators and potential danger.

They move silently by walking on the tips of their toes.

That's what I've been told. So maybe you need dogs,

if you want to hunt coyotes.

The coyote hunters have put on

the camouflage of righteousness.

I got into a conversation with my mechanic.

A nice guy. He closes the shop during deer season.

He told me it's impossible to kill too many coyotes—

there are so many of them, and anyway,

shoot them all and we'd be better off.

I couldn't help thinking that beneath

all the bad things to be said about coyotes,

killing fawns and so on,

he doesn't like the competition.

The hunters say they are performing a public service,

heading off the scourge of coyotes.

But I don't think they get up and go out in the early cold

in order to keep the deer population at a proper level.

I wish they would acknowledge sometimes

that they get some deep satisfaction from shooting things.

Well, hunting is as natural for men as for coyotes.

And hunters are the ones who sit out in the cold and silence,

and know how to put meat on the table,

and where it comes from.

I don't really want to criticize.

I admire the skill, and the being out in the cold.

But doesn't it become grotesque,

when the technology gets too sophisticated?

The technology of coyotes is something else.

Sense of smell sharpened to a keenness,

superb wariness, teeth, lean strength,

marvelous patience and opportunism.

Sophisticated is the wrong word for radio collars.

It's the technology of coyotes

that deserves to be called sophisticated.

My friend over in Vermont lets his neighbors hunt

in his woods during deer season.

This year he noticed a small drag mark in the snow,

and he asked his neighbor about it.

The neighbor admitted he'd shot a coyote.

My friend told him not to do it again.

The neighbor didn't ask why not.

He just apologized, a little sheepish, and said he wouldn't.

I asked my friend why he's protecting coyotes.

"I don't know," he said. "I like having them out there.

I like hearing them sing in the night, especially in winter."

Music of coyotes in the depths of a winter night.

Four-legged hunters and singers, devoted to their families,

making their way through deep snow.

POETRY GATHERING ON THE HILL

So here's the scene: a poetry gathering

on a beautiful September day, on a hill,

At the homestead of one of the poets.

Some woods behind the house,

but for the other 300 degrees,

an amazing vista spreading away—

rolling slopes, then ridge after ridge of fields and woods

in the blazing cool sunlight.

Just beyond where we can see, there are lakes, big ones.

You can feel them out there.

Early September. End of summer. Fall about to happen.

A party tent has been set up.

It flaps and shifts in the breezy day.

About fifty people have come.

If you put out an invitation for a poetry reading,

and make part of the program

an open reading, when anyone can read a poem,

you're likely to get fifty poets.

And a potluck supper afterward doesn't hurt.

But first, a reading by the headliner,

a somewhat well-known, not to say famous, poet.

He has a bit of an international reputation—

he'll be leaving for Italy in a couple of days,

with a one-way ticket, he says.

So here's the scene: He is sitting at a table—

because he can't stand up, because he hurt his foot,

he dropped a bookcase on it, he says—

as he begins reading, something starts to happen

that didn't have anything to do with him.

The driveway leading to the poet's house

is a long farm lane, maybe a quarter mile,

that swoops in around the hilltop

before it goes into a long straight stretch

up to the house. And as he sits reading,

there appears in the distance, coming around that long curve,

a large, horse-drawn wagon. And soon we can see

that it is loaded with firewood, and that the horses

are three, big brown work horses. At pulled-by-horses pace,

it takes several minutes for it to approach,

but approach it does, and as it draws closer

we can see that one of the horses, the one in the middle,

is even bigger than the others, it's enormous,

and also that the wagon

is being driven by three boys—

actually just one boy holds the reins,

the tallest, the one in the middle.

The tallest, but he can't be more than fifteen.

And as the poet goes on reading,

on they come, wagon, wagonload

of split firewood, dark horses, boys,

Amish, in their straw hats.

And the poet has no idea

of what is approaching behind him,

but everyone in the audience

can't not see it,

this slow stately thing.

So when the wagon finally pulls up

beside the tent

and in its solid wagon glory, stops,

the poet looks over and realizes

what has happened, and gracefully says,

"Well, nobody heard that poem,"

and if he is right about anything in his poems today,

he is right about that.

The poet whose house it is

goes over and talks to the boys,

and he says to us under the tent,

"We weren't expecting them just now."

After a minute or two the wagon moves on

to where it is to be unloaded,

and through the rest of the poet's reading

there is the clunking sound of the logs

being tossed off the wagon making a pile.

After a while, the rhythmic clunking stops.

and the wagon goes off

in horse-drawn silence, departing another way.

After the featured poet, there is a short break,

and the open reading begins. We read to each other

for quite a while, more than an hour,

and there are some good poems read,

and it is good to sit listening to them

under the windy tent of September. But clearly

the most memorable poem of the day is the wagon,

the ponderous, graceful horses, and the boys,

in their halo straw hats, coming slowly down the lane.

JIMI HENDRIX

My freshman year of college, fall 1965,

one of the first things that happened

was a concert in the Student Union. I was amazed,

because it was the Isley Brothers. I was a big fan.

If you know anything about rock & roll,

or maybe I should say rhythm & blues,

the former just recently at that time

born out of the latter, and the two of them

talking to each other in a wonderful explosion—

if you remember that musical moment,

you know the Isley Brothers

for their great record "Shout," Parts I and II,

which, speaking personally, which is what I am doing,

hit my teen-aged ears like a revelation—

the wildest song I had ever heard.

And it did make me want to shout, and even now

I do shout now and then,

though mostly, in my case, it is an inner shout.

It's still in there, though I am

at the other end of life now.

Thank God I can still be moved

by "Shout" when I hear it.

It must mean I am still alive

The Isley Brothers had another big hit

soon after that, "Twist and Shout,"

another wonderful song.

I always liked their version

better than the Beatles',

which came along a year or so later.

But that's another story.

So there I was, a freshman in college,

and the Isley Brothers being there,

on stage, in person,

gave me the impression

that this place must really exist,

and also that perhaps

I was where I was supposed to be,

which was very much an open question

at that point. There they were,

Ronald, Rudolph, and O'Kelly,

singing and dancing and shouting,

and I was standing right in front of the stage.

And there was a band behind them, pumping away.

And in that band there was a guitar player,

who looked a little strange.

His hair was longer than the others' —

a straightened straggly nest.

He was wearing a back-up band suit

like the others, but you could tell

there was something different about him.

Especially you could tell

when the Isley Brothers cut him some slack

and let him take some solos,

and he not only played, he started playing

with his teeth, and then behind his back.

The Isley Brothers were great,

they did not disappoint.

But it was pretty clear, if anything was clear,

that something else was going on with the guitar player.

At intermission I rushed back

to my dorm room, and got my Isley Brothers LP.

Things must have been more relaxed in those days,

because I had no trouble getting backstage.

I just walked through the door, and there I was,

and I walked over to the Isley Brothers

and asked them to sign my album.

Which they were pleased to do.

I remember Ronald saying,

when I handed it to him, "Well, all right."

If you don't believe

Any of this I'm telling you,

I can show you the album,

with their autographs written

in blue ballpoint pen

across their sharp white suits.

But the thing is, on my way to the Isley Brothers,

I walked right past the guitar player,

who was leaning against the wall, smoking a cigarette.

He looked sullen, as I recall.

I could have stopped and complimented him

on his playing, asked for his autograph,

but I didn't. But as I like to say

when I tell this story, as I have done many times,

I was as close to Jimi Hendrix as I am to you.

It was not long after that that he hit it big,

and joined the explosion

of young musicians happening then—

group after group, album after album.

I don't need to name them all,

but it was amazing. Yet at the same time,

we took it for granted, and felt it was ours, the brilliance….

We were, to put it mildly, a little spoiled .

Among all that burst of talent and excitement,

Jimi Hendrix stands out—don't you think? Nobody like him.

I bought his first single, which was actually a double,

because how could you choose between "Purple Haze"

and "The Wind Cries Mary"?

The thudding primal beat of the former,

the ethereal guitar wail of the latter, so moody and mournful.

I've always especially liked when he would

take someone else's song, tipping his hat,

and make it wildly his own.

"All Along the Watchtower," oh, that's a good one.

"Sgt. Pepper's Lonely Hearts Club Band."

"Wild Thing," "Johnny B. Goode" — and of course

his incredible rendition, astonishing really,

of "The Star-Spangled Banner."

Was he excessive

in his use of feedback? Maybe.

In his use of the wah-wah pedal?

No, I guess he used it just enough.

It was excessive though

when he set his guitar on fire

and kneeled over it

deliriously squirting

lighter fluid into the flames.

One should not destroy one's instrument.

It's not like I've been listening to Jimi Hendrix

non-stop for fifty years.

My box of vinyl has survived,

but it's in the attic.

Maybe one of my kids will want it.

But I heard by chance the other day

"Foxy Lady," and it still sounded great.

So I went to the library

and got out some CD's.

"Little Wing," I'd forgotten that one,

I might never have heard it again,

which would have been too bad, wonderful song,

I was much moved by it, the way

his guitar floated and soared.

Have you heard that little coda

he put at the end of "Bold as Love" lately?

He didn't live long.

Not surprising, so much frenzy,

too much high flying, too many drugs

to mix with his virtuosity.

"Music is my religion," he said.

No doubt many musicians have said that, or felt it,

but he had more alleluias than most, and it's a nice detail

that fate arranged, that he lived for a while

in the same house in London where Handel once lived.

FRANKENSTEIN

James Whale

was a genius. He didn't want

to be known only as

a director of horror films,

but when you make a work of art

as perfect as *Frankenstein* (1931),

and then you are given the job

of making a sequel,

and you manage to make one

that is even greater

than the first film,

what can you expect?

The critics seem to think that

about *The Bride of Frankenstein* (1935),

but personally, I don't see why we need to choose.

Is Van Gogh's "Self-Portrait with Bandaged Ear"

greater than his "Wheatfield with Crows"?

But, James Whale was a genius,

based on those two great *Frankensteins*.

They were already old movies when I was a kid,

eleven or twelve years old,

watching them on TV late at night.

My parents were permissive

in that way. And those old films were intense

in the living room

where my friend Tom and I

watched with the lights out,

and the tree limbs were moving shadows

in the light of the streetlight

on Fairview Avenue on a windy night.

Though both are great,

the first film was the scarier of the two,

because of its austerity.

I wouldn't have used the word "austerity" then,

but on later viewings,

that seems to be the word for it.

In *The Bride*, Whale

was fooling around a little,

exaggerating his effects, having some fun.

The first film was so pure,

so gaunt and hollow-cheeked.

The Bride has music,

a wonderful score actually, with a different theme

for each of the main characters,

while the first film has no music,

but a lot of silence.

In *The Bride*, the monster's sensitivity

was developed more— for example in the part

where he finds happiness for a little while

living with the blind hermit in the woods.

It's the only time, I think, in all the many Frankenstein films

that have been made, good or bad,

that we get to see the monster smoking a cigar.

Even a kid could feel

the poignancy of their life together in the hermit's hut.

"Friend—good," the monster said.

And the bride? What should she look like?

Who would have expected

that she would be beautiful?—

though in a very bizarre way,

with her neck sutures

and amazing electrified hair.

The wedding scene is fantastic,

the tableau of the wedding party

in the lab in the old stone tower—

then the peal of wedding bells, evoking the hope

of all weddings. But then

the couple are introduced to one another

and it is quickly clear

that the match won't work.

She hisses at him, he sees how it is,

and he blows the place up.

You could see the monster's humanity

in the first film too,

but it was more subtle.

Check out the scene

when the monster first enters.

He comes in walking backward.

An amazing detail.

I'm guessing it was James Whale who came up with it.

"Boris, try coming in walking backward."

It is so weird. Why would he do that?

And when he turns, we are given

several silent seconds

from a couple of angles,

to take in his face.

Incredible. Austere.

Then Dr. Frankenstein (the wonderful Colin Clive)

gets him to sit down.

He opens the skylight, the monster looks up,

stands up, reaches up toward the light.

They quickly close the skylight.

The monster is disappointed, perplexed.

It's a beautiful piece of acting.

Just then the hunchback assistant

(the wonderful Dwight Frye)

comes in with his god-damned torch

and threatens the monster with it, gratuitous cruelty,

and the lingering moment

of uplifted hands is shattered.

Beseeching hands of the monster again

in the scene by the lake

where he encounters the little girl

who gives him flowers,

and then confusion overtakes him,

and he throws her in the lake, she will drown…

and the monster knows again that in this world

nothing is going to go well for him,

a terrible realization that others have had as well.

Isn't it strange that they didn't give him a name?

Eventually he became known by his maker's,

but from the start he is known as, "the monster."

How would that feel, to always be referred to as

"the monster"?

I don't want to sentimentalize.

He does kill people now and then.

In the scene where he comes in through the window

and stalks Dr. Frankenstein's bride,

who is alone in her bedroom, he is hideous,

coming up silently behind her…

he is, as we say, a nightmare.

Cinema is a collaborative art,

and I don't know how to sort out exactly

what the director does

from what the actors do,

from what the screenwriter does…

it's all woven together.

And what the make-up person does —

in this case, the make-up person

was some kind of genius too.

The set designer? The cameraman?

And of course Mary Shelley, a young woman

hanging out with egomaniacal poets

a hundred years before, is in there too.

Boris Karloff? I can still hear

his snarl, see the clumsy power

of his flailing arms in the dungeon,

in the flames of the windmill.

Still see the crushing of his hopeful smile

when his bride-to-be recoils.

Thank you, Boris.

Thank you, James Whale.

And all the others

who contributed and collaborated.

And the frightening, beautiful monster.

FALCON PARK

24

Minor league. Class A. Auburn Doubledays

vs. the Batavia Muckdogs. Very young guys

hoping to make it.

Small crowd. Maybe 500 tonight.

A perfect summer evening.

The Doubledays' shortstop is having a rough night.

He makes excellent stops, going right,

going left, but then

throws wide or high. One went into the stands.

Four errors, all throwing. He must feel terrible.

But his errant throws, and his suffering,

are not enough to keep me

from enjoying this cool July evening

in the stands, the crack of the bat,

the baseball ambience of well-being.

The pitchers throw hard.

How beautiful the swift passage of the ball

from mound to plate,

the emphatic firm simplicity

of the catcher catching.

Lots of contact tonight.

Not a lot of walks, or called strikes,

so the crack of the bat

echoes satisfactorily

through the night air often.

Line-drives. Also flyballs,

which suits me. I've always especially enjoyed

the way outfielders move, arrive standing waiting

for that long trajectory to come to them, to the precise

only spot of the glove in the whole spacious night.

Running catches a kind of ecstasy,

the amazing smoothness of loping and taking it out of the air,

or leaping, spearing the ball near the top of the fence—or

the ball out of reach, sailing above them

majestically over the wall.

So, a beautiful night for baseball—

and I like observing the fans

almost as much as the game.

A motley bunch, with our logos,

with our food and beer,

with our egos, our ballpark calm—

with our boredom punctuated by excitement,

pleasure of a good play. And the young couple

a couple of rows in front of me, with two little boys,

learning the atmosphere that will serve them well later,

and the way they seem to be happy together.

The husband and wife lean into each other.

Now he says something to her, into her ear

lost under her long black hair, and she looks at him

with something like disapproval and something like a smile,

and gives him a sexy little affectionate punch in the arm.

THE CROWS FLY INTO TOWN AT DUSK

Around four o'clock or so they begin drifting in.
The couple walking in the cemetery
where the stones flow from other centuries along the hills

notice how the silence gives way to a few caws,
and then more and more coast in from somewhere,
raucous chorus, a steady, uneven stream

flowing in and gathering in the bare
tall old trees. The man sitting in the dentist's chair
waiting for the dentist to appear,

stares out the window
and sees the crows riding the air,
flapping and descending, sifting

into the trees across the street,
a haunting sight he hadn't expected here.
Someone driving west through town is amazed

at the swirl of the flock across the winter sky,
hundreds, thousands, across clouds
stirred in cold blazing orange and pink.

Wow, a natural wonder, he thinks,

the most beautiful thing he's ever seen

in this city, or maybe anywhere, and he feels

it's good luck to live in a place where there are crows, so many,

a symposium of crows, a séance, a rendezvous—something

to be grateful for, to share the wintry earth with crows.

SIGNS ALONG THE ROAD

There's a migration into the county where I live.

Mennonites are coming to upstate New York from Pennsylvania.

They're keeping some small farms going.

Bless them—it isn't easy.

Maybe you need to be deeply religious to do it.

I've gotten to know a few of them—

our neighbors half-a-mile up the road,

and the roofers who put on our new metal roof.

People as nice and helpful as you could want to meet.

When my wife and I are driving to church,

we pass many cars and vans, black or gray,

with Mennonite families headed to theirs.

Bearded men, women wearing little lace bonnets, lots of kids.

They look serious—as my wife and I probably do too

through our windshield—the serious look

of couples in cars, people on the way to church.

You can tell which houses are theirs,

which trailers and double-wides,

because it is their practice to put small signs,

brown with yellow lettering, out near the mailbox,

with brief messages for passers-by.

Sometimes it's wisdom: "Tribulation worketh patience."

Sometimes it's a leading question:

"Is Jesus the shepherd of your life?"

Sometimes it's a warning: "Turn every one away

from thy evil way."

Sometimes the judgment is more indirect:

"With Christ life is worth living" —

the kind of thing that annoys my Jewish friends.

Sometimes the judgment is more blunt:

"Adulterers God will judge."

At the moment, the sign I drive past every day says,

"Sorrow shall be to the wicked" on one side,

and "The wicked shall perish" on the other.

Which makes me wonder, who the wicked are,

and whether my new neighbors consider me one of them.

And I wonder whether I might actually be.

"The Lord Jesus Christ is coming—are you ready?"

I really don't know if I am.

For a while there was on one side of a sign,

"Husbands—love your wives," and on the other,

"Wives—submit unto your husbands" —

one thought heading east, one heading west.

Sometimes it's simply gratitude or praise:

"Unto God we give thanks," or "Count your blessings," or

"The Lord is great and greatly to be praised."

I read these bits of creed and faith and judgment

along the road and think about them.

But the one that shocked me

was the announcement that appeared one morning:

"The earth shall be burned up."

I'm always sorry to hear such news.

The blue planet, unimaginably old,

our home, spinning slowly,

consigned to the flames, and in so calm a voice.

To make matters worse, this sign

was displayed at a farm.

A beautiful little dairy operation,

not one of those humongous factory-like places.

Their cows still get out on the pasture—

the black and white of Holsteins,

and one lustrous brown horse among them.

I feel like stopping and telling them

how much better it would be

if they replaced "The earth shall be burned up"

with the large yellow one they have

outside their small processing plant

down in the village, where from the storefront

a polite and friendly young woman in a long dress

sells their excellent milk, and butter, and yogurt, and cheese and eggs,

out of the cool of the coolers.

It would be a much better

message to see along the road,

and personally I think better theology as well:

"Our cows and hens enjoy grazing."

JAMES BROWN

James Brown's son came to town,

to give a talk and do a book-signing at the local bookstore.

He's written a book about his father,

good timing, it coincides with the new movie

about James Brown's life.

He says he hasn't seen it,

but he knows it's far from true.

And now he's out on tour, a different kind of show

than James Brown's. He must be a good musician—

he played in James Brown's band for several years. But it appears

that now he's somewhat down on his luck,

or why would he be here in Auburn, New York,

in this little bookstore, peddling his book.

He says that if he'd known how hard it is being an author,

he probably wouldn't have written it.

He's casually dressed, jeans, t-shirt, running shoes,

skinny braids hanging down

from under a sort of narrow-brimmed black cowboy hat.

Apparently he hasn't inherited his father's sense of style.

He's probably about fifty. He's got a paunch.

He's an ordinary looking, middle-aged guy.

But he's James Brown's son, and he's come to town,

and fifty or so people have filled the folding chairs,

and as he paces around the area

where the book racks have been pushed aside,

he does a good job talking about his dad.

He acknowledges he wasn't the most attentive father,

and that he didn't always treat his mother very well,

but he speaks of him with, I think,

honesty, respect, and love.

And every now and then he says,

"James Brown—there was something

divine about that man."

He talks a lot about how hard his father's childhood was—

abandoned by his mother, who left

because she was afraid of his father, who was a rough man,

and who James Brown worshipped.

Extreme poverty, living in a shack, prison early on.

"He came to those distorted conceptions

of human relationships honestly," he says.

"Living in survival mode makes for a lifetime of bad decisions,"

he says. "Though I am much larger

than my father, I always knew he could whip my ass

if I ever crossed the line," he says.

He talks about what a hard-driving boss

his father was, maniacally controlling,

all the musicians who ever worked with him say the same.

"You had to be on top of your game at all times."

"Every instrument a drum"

was one of his principles and demands,

and listening to his greatest songs

it's clear he got what he was after.

I don't really have the language for it, but I'd say

that some of those songs aren't even songs

exactly—they're chants, they're dances in the air.

"I Got You/ I Feel Good," for example.

From the first moment/scream to the last,

its rhythms are so tight,

so beautifully spasmodic,

you'd almost have to be dead

not to move to it.

That's how good we're supposed to feel,

isn't it?

I saw James Brown in person, it must have been 1967,

in Harrisburg, Pennsylvania. My college friends and I

were the only white people in the audience, or close to it.

And it was a great show. I saw James Brown

do his famous cape routine. "Please Please Please,"

falling again and again to his knees,

getting up, running back, unable to leave the stage.

I wasn't alive in Leipzig in 1725,

so I didn't get to hear Bach play the organ,

and I didn't live in the Australian outback

in all those millennia before time got sliced in half

with BCE and CE, so I'm sure I missed

some great didgeridoo players,

but living in America in the second half of the 20th century,

I got to see James Brown live on stage,

and fifty years later, I guess it is still

one of the greatest things I've ever seen.

His son talks about what a positive force he was,

all through the shifting tides and turmoil of those times.

"He was more civil rights than civil rights," he says.

He prevented a few riots in his time.

Who else could sing message songs

like "Don't Be a Drop-out"

and still seem like the wildest man around?

When he put out "Say It Loud, I'm Black and I'm Proud,"

one of my psychedelically oriented friends said,

"Well, you won't be able to sing along with that one,"

but it was such a good song, call and response,

that I did sing it to myself now and then

as I walked across campus under the tall liberal arts trees.

I didn't follow his music over the next few decades.

I would read about him in the newspaper

when there was a story about him—usually his troubles

with the IRS, his wives, the law.

Somehow I missed it when he sang duets with Pavarotti—

one of many things I heard about when I read his son's book.

But whenever I heard one of his old songs on the radio,

those irresistible rhythms, those crisp horns,

the wonderful rawness of his voice,

wherever I was, I did a little dance.

At the end of the talk, James Brown's son took out a guitar

and offered to do one of his father's songs.

Someone asked for the obvious choice:

"Papa's Got a Brand-New Bag."

So he thought for a few seconds, and then started to pick it out,

and he seemed to take special pleasure

when he got to the measure

when the band stops and the guitar rapidly strums—

deedle-eedle-eedle-eet!

But at one point, he forgot the lyrics, and paused, and asked,

"What's the next line?" and I'm proud to say,

not black and proud, but proud nonetheless,

that it was me who provided the next line: "It's out of sight."

And James Brown's son thanked me, and he finished

his sweet, acoustic version of his father's great song.

And then he said good night.

"How can we tell the dancer from the dance?"

"Every instrument a drum."

"Try Me." "Cold Sweat." "I Feel Good."

James Brown—there was something divine about that man.

PIZZA

No shortage of pizzerias

in Auburn, New York,

or in most cities and towns in America today.

And of course you can get a slice

in any convenience store.

It wasn't so long ago, maybe fifty years,

pizzerias were just arriving.

As I remember it, there was

something exotic about them,

and there was a certain craftsmanly aura.

In Auburn, the most venerable pizzeria

is Angelo's. Founded by Angelo—Angelo D'Angelo.

Not a franchise. Only one store, never more,

though the location changed

when urban renewal came to town

in the sixties and seventies

and knocked whole blocks of buildings down,

and a four-lane highway, known as "the arterial,"

even though it drained most of the life-blood

from downtown. For a long time,

half the stores stood empty.

Lately, there's been a come-back,

and even if the empty stores

are mostly lawyer's offices, pawn shops, and tattoo parlors,

at least more of them are filled.

Some businesses continued

through all those changes, just a few,

and one of those is Angelo's.

He went on making pizzas

year after year, decade after decade,

and when he sold the business a few years ago,

he stuck around—as a consultant, I suppose.

To my grandsons, he's a sort of celebrity,

also maybe an historical exhibit.

Whenever they come to visit,

they want to go for lunch at Angelo's.

I'm happy to oblige them.

We come through the door and order

our pizza from the young woman

standing between the register and the oven.

And if we are lucky, Angelo will be there too.

Today we are lucky.   He is standing

in front of the soda case, wearing his white apron.

A short, thick-torsoed man. We walk up to him.

I tell them to order their sodas.

Hard decision for kids whose parents

don't often allow them to have soda.

And at the same time, to be asking for the soda

from this old man. They make their choices,

Angelo hands us the cold cans

and says "There you go," and we go

and sit down at one of the tables, and pop them open.

Four tables. Red plastic table cloths.

On the back wall, there's a section of the sign

from the original store. It has an old Pepsi logo,

in the elegant cursive of an earlier time,

and to the right of Pepsi, the words

"Angelo's," and "5 min. take out."

One way to pass the time

while waiting for one's pizza

is to count the pizza boxes stacked against the wall.

I teach the boys trick of counting

just one pile and multiplying

by the number of stacks.

I do the multiplication on a napkin.

It comes out to a pretty impressive number.

Pretty soon, the pizza arrives.

And again we are lucky. Angelo himself serves us.

A long time since he left Italy,

but he still has his accent.

He places the pizza on the aluminum pedestal,

and with his large metal spatula,

he gives us each a slice

on our double paper plates.

And he says in a friendly but not effusive way,

"Take-a your time. Don't eat too fast."

I tell him "Thanks." I tell him the kids

always want to eat here when they come to visit,

and he smiles, and says, "It's-a the best."

I ask him, "Angelo, how many pizzas

do you think you've made?"

He laughs a little and says, "Only God knows."

There's something serious

about the way he says it.

If he had said, "God only knows,"

it would have sounded like a cliché,

but the way he says it, it seems thoughtful,

with philosophical, perhaps spiritual, significance.

Or so it seems to me. More personal maybe?

"Only God knows."

In any case, he doesn't know,

but the pizza is excellent— delicious, hot,

a beautiful molten red-orange sun,

and we are orbiting around it, and eating it

in large floppy slices. And standing

right over there, hands folded behind his back,

rocking back and forth on his heels,

lost in thought, the man himself,

the lord of pizza, Angelo.

BEER

Drinking beer is more complicated than it used to be.

The craft beer movement, with all its local breweries,

all producing their own unique brews, and the microbreweries

attached to restaurants—it's impossible to keep track of them all,

let alone sample all those beers and ales. Our small city

has two breweries of its own now. One is Prison City

Pub and Brewery, named for New York's oldest prison,

which sits with its 30 foot walls right in the middle of town.

It's a pleasure perusing the beer list, trying to choose.

How about the one that is "Hazy yellow

with aromas of tropical and citrus fruits, peach and pine,"

or the one that is

"a crisp, American style wheat beer

with raspberry puree added after filtration,

giving it a subtle purple color,

fruity aroma, and tartly sweet taste"?

This is just beer we're talking about.

I'm going with Baby Face Nelson,

"a light bodied beer exclusively hopped

with Nelson Sauvin, giving it lemon white wine

aromas and flavors of roasted lemon

and passion fruit, and a dry finish."

When it comes in its beer goblet, it is delicious.

All this makes it hard to stay loyal

to the old fashioned brands.

I love the green bottles

of Heineken and Rolling Rock.

And Stella Artois, where they've been making beer

for six hundred years.

Drinking from the bottle is fine.

but pouring carefully from bottle to glass

is a pleasure in itself….

But beer from the tap, coming to the table

in curvaceous glass, or frosted mug?

Maybe they're serving Molson or Labatt's.

I have no problem with that,

I can even enjoy a Budweiser,

though my beer-snob friends look at me askance.

Then there's also the issue of shopping local.

Most of those old familiar brands

are owned now by something called InBev,

a huge multinational corporation,

trying to crush the opposition

and take all the shelf space for themselves.

But they don't seem to be succeeding,

judging by the supermarket where I shop,

which has a beer aisle that is about a block long,

so many beers you could graze for hours,

trying to choose. Flat Tire. Flying Dog.

Aunt Sally. Magic Hat. Middle Ages.

All Day IPA. Flower Power. Full Sail.

Long Trail. Caged Alpha Monkey. Smuttynose.

But as far as local goes, just a couple of blocks

from Prison City, perched on top of a 4-story building,

a sign with big letters, all caps:

GENESEE BEER.

For fifty years it's looked silently down

over our comings and goings,

a great, benevolent artwork,

purer than anything by Andy Warhol.

The beer made over in Rochester, not very far away….

The sign's poetic style is a far cry

from Prison City's descriptions.

I like them both, though I think

I prefer the sign's.

It's lit up red at night.

Simplicity. That's the thing.

The simplicity of having a cold one.

All I intended to say was, I agree with Ben Franklin,

who said, "Beer is proof that God loves us,

and wants us to be happy."

Praise for the sense of equanimity

that comes as you dip your lip

into the foam, and take a long sip.

The pleasant sensation

of it going down your throat.

And the slightest buzz

after having one, or two.

MORNING MASS

I've been going to mass lately. I'm not a Catholic,

but a friend of mine is in a nursing home now.

He lived in an old house that belonged to his parents.

He grew up there. In his twenties, he had a breakdown.

He'd gone to college, he was teaching high school

in New York City, but when he started hearing voices,

he couldn't teach any longer, and he came back home.

He moved back in with his parents,

and when they died, he lived in the house alone.

He didn't drive a car. The first time he drove solo,

he had an accident, and he never drove again.

He rode a bicycle. You would see him

even on the coldest days, pedaling along,

his face red in the bicycle wind.

After a few years he applied to teach

in the local school district, but

"they wouldn't have me," he says,

without anger, with perfect matter-of-factness.

He took courses at the community college.

That's where I met him. He took every

literature and writing course we offered.

In Creative Writing, he wrote poems

so flat they had a kind of beauty.

He didn't have to learn what we always tell them,

not to use flowery language.

I don't think he ever used a metaphor.

Later, he wrote some plays,

four or five pages long, remarkable

for their almost total lack of drama.

He wasn't trying to imitate Samuel Beckett,

but in a way he outdid him.

He is a devotee of literature, and philosophy,

though I can never tell what he takes

from the great books he reads,

other than that they are great.

When we've talked over eggs at the diner,

he never says much beyond

an expression of admiration—

"Wherever it is you are going,

Shakespeare has already been there," he says,

quoting an eminent critic. That's as far as he'll go.

But he keeps on reading, and listening to *Great Courses*.

And he has religion. He doesn't say "goodbye"

or "so long," he always says,

"The peace of the Lord be with you."

I'm sure it was mass he was coming from,

when I'd see him on his bicycle in the morning.

But now he's in his seventies,

he has chronic pulmonary disorder

from all his years of smoking.

His bicycling days are over.

And when he fell and broke his hip,

the house was sold, and it was

the adult care facility for him.

I knew how deeply Catholic he is—

some of the plays he showed me were about saints.

And he had one about Teilhard de Chardin.

When I asked him if he'd like me

to pick him up for mass, he accepted immediately.

So now we go once or twice a week.

To me the mass is an enigmatic performance.

I go through the motions, sitting and rising.

I listen, I recognize the readings.

I listen to the priest's words, and the murmur of responses.

My friend knows what to say.

I join in on the Lord's Prayer. I know that one.

But I do not take communion. I sit and watch the people

receive the thin biscuit of the body of Christ.

Once I asked him what he gets from the mass.

"What do you feel? Is it emotional?"

"No, there's really not any emotion. It's just to go,

and to know that the Lord died for our sins,

and we have salvation through him."

The other day, as we drove back to the nursing home,

having again watched the priest, a man his age,

lead the mass, the handler of mysteries,

I asked him if he had ever wanted to be a priest.

Yes, he said. When he was a kid he thought he might.

And then when he was about forty, living the life

that was his life, he thought again

that he might try for the priesthood,

there was a special program for late-arrivers, but

"They wouldn't have me," he said.

Seemingly without anger. With saint-like acceptance.

SUBWAY GOSPEL SINGERS

Into the car from the next car

through the opening and shutting door

that when it opens raises the level

of subway noise, and when it shuts

restores the normal clatter—through the door

came two elderly, shabby men.

They stood a moment, then one said,

"Ladies and gentlemen, we are gospel singers.

There used to be three of us.

One member of our group has passed away,

but we are carrying on as best we can.

We would like to sing for you, and we hope that you

will show some love." By which he meant,

not just love, but putting some money

in the tall styrofoam cup he held in his hand.

And with that, they sang, a swinging, upbeat number.

It was about Jesus. He marked time

with the hand not holding the cup,

his fingers slightly curved, but pointing out ahead of him,

moving up and down.

The other singer kept his eyes downturned

while he sang harmony, a beautiful bass.

Everyone else seemed to be ignoring them,

but I took out my wallet and got up

and put a ten dollar bill in the cup.

I thought that wasn't bad for a subway donation.

I wanted to express my appreciation.

The singer with the cup looked down into it,

and nodded to me, a courtly nod. I was hoping

for a longer concert, I would have liked

to listen to them all the way to the Battery,

but no, as the train slowed,

they walked down to the other end of the car,

still singing, and when the doors opened

the verse had ended, and they walked through.

Maybe I should have given them twenty.

What's the right price for a subway choir?

Two shabby men singing

like angels singing like shabby men,

never to be seen again.

ARMED HIKER

Out on the Loyalsock Trail, in the mountains of northern Pennsylvania,

I'm hiking a few miles on a perfect, cool fall day.

And while I'm standing at the top of a waterfall

just below an amazing stretch of crumbling sandstone cliffs, 30 feet tall,

watching the water splash over the dark rocks,

listening to the steady, spattering sound

that make you feel like you're

a hundred thousand years old, but in a good way,

someone else hiking alone

is coming up the ravine.

A young guy, probably in his twenties.

He's lean, muscular.

His pack is large, he's using walking poles,

he's got a red bandanna tied around his head.

He's moving right along.

But he stops and we say hello.

I wouldn't call him cheerful.

He doesn't smile. He's serious.

"Beautiful day. How far are you going?" I say.

He's doing the whole trail. Fifty-nine miles.

I notice that his equipment includes a pistol,

strapped to the middle of his chest.

It's in a holster, but it's not concealed. It gleams silver.

Hmm, what's the proper etiquette?

Do I say, "Nice pistol"?

For some reason I don't ask, and after a couple minutes,

we say, "Have a good one," "You too,"

and he heads off again, striding along on his poles.

Now that he's gone, I wish I hadn't acted

as if the gun weren't there.

I wish I'd asked him about it.

There are definitely bears in these mountains,

but I've hiked here forty years, and only run into one once,

and it went the other way, off into the woods.

What was it that he was thinking he might need to shoot?

It might have been an interesting conversation,

in the cool ancient room of the waterfall.

ECCENTRIC FRIEND

What we have in common is old horror movies,

in particular, the classics, from the great period

of the 1930s. You have to go back

past many sequels, parodies, and Halloween costumes

to get to the originals in all their purity.

Frankenstein, and *The Bride of Frankenstein.*

Son of Frankenstein, too.

The monster was starting on his way

to becoming the flat character he became in that one.

But it introduced Bela Lugosi's character Igor,

wonderful with his broken neck.

And of course *Dracula,* also Bela Lugosi,

making his greatest contribution

to making the collective unconscious conscious,

turning a piece of it into a caped gentleman

who speaks English with a Hungarian accent.

And *WereWolf of London, The Mummy, The Invisible Man.* And

certain lesser known films, like *The Raven* and *The Black Cat,*

those two featuring both Bela Lugosi and Boris Karloff—

movies superb in their sublime melodrama.

And *The Old Dark House.*

And *Island of Lost Souls.*

My wife is my main movie-watching companion,

but for some reason she has no interest

in watching those old films.

But I have a friend who is a fan. You could say, a devotee.

We don't know each other well,

but we see each other now and then. Usually,

at the supermarket. I don't think he has a car.

Whenever I see him, he's on foot.

He has an intent, straight-ahead gaze

as he walks along the street.

He seems absorbed in thought.

Years ago, he took a course I used to teach,

Film & Literature.   Because the syllabus included

Dr. Jekyll and Mr. Hyde, a certain friendship

developed between us. When we run

into each other, we stop and talk.

I could ask him whether he has a car or not,

but we don't go into such personal details.

No, we talk about movies, usually those old ones

we both for some reason, or reasons, love.

Lately, we've started exchanging occasional emails.

Short reviews and recommendations, bits of film lore.

For example, after revisiting *The Raven*

for the first time in fifty years,

I did a little research, and I told him

a detail I'd found about Lugosi.

Once when he was attending a revival screening

in the 1950s, when he was not long for this world,

in the middle of the film Bela rose from his seat and said,

"God, I was a handsome bastard in those days!"

My friend replied: "Yes, he was a handsome bastard.

What a genius acting style, like no other.

I wonder how he would have done

if the almighty studios had given him a chance

with A-list pictures, opposite Gable, Cagney,

Bette Davis and the like. I wonder

if he would have been such a helpless, hopeless

tragic figure and addict. How would he have done,

given leading man romantic roles?

He certainly was successful as a Hollywood lady's man

and he was a good-looking until drugs

and who knows what else (depression?)

ravaged him. I found a picture

of the nude Clara Bow painting he kept over his bed.

It recently sold at auction for $30,000.

If I had the cash, I would have bought it."

He attached the painting. I could see what he meant.

I had mentioned that it's hard to find time

to watch all the movies that one might want to watch,

and after his praise of Lugosi, my friend said,

"I understand having 'so much to watch.'

I own at least a thousand DVDs. I will never see them all.

But believe it or not, at night when I am all settled

and ready to watch a film, sometimes

I cannot decide what to watch.

Not because there are so many I can't make up my mind,

but rather nothing looks good enough for my mood.

I have looked at them for nearly an hour sometimes,

and will go to bed without having watched

anything at all." And then, though his name is Robert Brewer,

he signed the message, "Robert Brewgosi."

My good luck, to have such an eccentric friend.

HENRY THOREAU AND ELLEN SEWALL

From Walter Harding, *The Days of Henry Thoreau*, Chapter Six

I can't stop thinking about some of these stories

from 19th century American literature,

lives long ago, but close enough that these people

seem very real in their dark clothes.

Because some of them wrote so well, the whole

territory of time feels still alive.

For example, the story

of Thoreau and Ellen Sewall.

They'd known each other before,

but they were only children then. And when

the Sewall family came to Concord in July, 1839,

for a two-week summer vacation, things were different.

She was seventeen now, and Henry twenty-two.

Oh, those are good ages. Can you remember

what seventeen and twenty-two were like?

And what the seventeen year old girl was like

when you were the shy twenty-two year old guy?

They spent a lot of time together in those two weeks,

though they were rarely if ever alone.

He took her for rides in his boat on the river,

though Aunt Prudence went along.

He took her to see the giraffe

that came to Concord on tour. A classic date.

I can picture them standing there

looking at the giraffe.

I remember going on dates like that.

And when the young people gathered

one of the things they did,

under the cover of an interest in phrenology,

was to feel each other's skulls.

It must have been exciting

putting your hands on the head of someone

of the opposite sex—

Henry, putting his hands on Ellen's hair,

feeling the lovely contours of her head.

No doubt he was trying to give her a compliment

when he said that her head had no bumps at all,

but the others who were there laughed,

because in phrenology no bumps would mean

that she was either a genius or an idiot.

Embarrassing for Thoreau.

Still, I like to think of those young people

feeling each other's heads.

The next summer, he apparently got her out in the boat alone,

and he played his flute for her as they drifted on the river.

He wrote in his journal:

"The other day I rowed in my boat a free,

even lovely young lady, and as I plied the oars,

she sat in the stern, and there was nothing but she

between me and the sky. So might all our lives

be picturesque if they were free enough."

Then he turned that into verse,

and sent her the poem:

"Up this pleasant stream let's row

   For the livelong summer's day,

Sprinkling foam where'er we go

   In wreaths as white as driven snow.

     Ply the oars! away! away!"

It's not "Wild nights—Wild nights!

Were I with thee

Wild nights should be

Our luxury!

Rowing in Eden—

Ah—the Sea!

Might I but moor—tonight—

In thee!"

But it's the same boat.

The problem was, Thoreau's brother John

was falling in love with her too,

and in a brotherly dynamic hard for us to understand,

the younger brother deferred to the older.

And Ellen accepted John's proposal at first,

maybe because she was too surprised to turn him down,

 but her parents were old-line conservative Unitarians,

and they wouldn't have her marrying into the Emersonian crowd—

and Ellen, meanwhile, decided that it was not John,

but Henry that she preferred.

This is all complex, and shadowy too, there are mysteries here

that will never be explained.

But after John was rejected, Henry proposed,

by letter, and then, after suspense

and more parental influence,

he was, by letter, turned down.

Later she said, "I never felt so badly

at sending a letter in my life."

But she turned him down.

She cut the pages from her diary

from that summer and fall.

But she missed a later entry

where she referred to the poem

about being in the boat on the river,

where she said, "That was the first

piece Henry gave me

in 'days long passed,' 'in years

not worth remembering.' I wonder

if his thoughts ever wander back

to those times when the hours sped so pleasantly

and we were so happy.

I think they do.

I little thought then

that he cared so much

as subsequent events have proved."

I don't mean to be overly curious

about other people's love lives,

but the truth is, Ellen Sewall was pretty,

in the daguerreotype from 1840,

with her long jaw, and her oddly bobbed hair

exposing her ear, and her slight smile

and her eyes gazing off to the side,

thinking of something else.

It's easy to see why she caught Henry's eye,

and John's eye, and others' eyes,

and the eye of the guy she married.

There are other details.

Years later, after Henry had died

she kept his picture on her living room wall.

I guess that's not so unusual—

she admired his writing.

On Henry's side, two months after the rejection, he wrote,

"To sigh under the cold, cold moon

for a love unrequited,

is to put a slight upon nature;

the natural remedy would be

to fall in love with the moon and night,

and find our love requited."

Which is pretty much what he did,

and how it worked out for him.

Two days later he wrote:

"Disappointment will make us conversant

with the nobler part of our nature."

He had long conversations

with the nobler part of his nature.

And that wasn't the end of it.

He saw Ellen occasionally for the rest of his life!

He knew her husband!

On a couple of occasions he took walks with him!

When Rev. Osgood came to preach in Concord once,

Henry didn't go to the service, of course,

but he did take the man who was married to Ellen

on a walk around Walden Pond.

But let's not exaggerate the cold side of his personality.

Let's give him credit for enormous dignity

and self-control that could break your heart.

And then there's the detail

that when he was dying

his sister mentioned Ellen's name, and he said,

"I have always loved her.

I have always loved her."

So many of Thoreau's words move me, and stay with me,

but none more than those.

OTIS REDDING

Wilson Pickett. Solomon Burke. Percy Sledge.

Sam and Dave. I was a fan

of all of them. And in

a slightly different wing, Levi Stubbs,

of The Four Tops, and David Ruffin,

of The Temptations, and in the silky

higher range, Smokey Robinson.

A little earlier, Sam Cooke, Jackie Wilson,

Fats Domino, Little Richard.

Not to mention James Brown,

a musical universe unto himself.

I've already written a poem about him.

Not to mention Ray Charles....

Soul Music—male division, 1960s.

It's a pleasure just to call their names.

I'm not sure about all that's happened since then.

Something happened

that caused me to lose touch.

But there's this period of a decade or so,

from which I can identify dozens of songs

from hearing just a few seconds,

sometimes it seems I can do it

from a single note.

I was in high school, then college.

For whatever reasons, my young soul

was wide open to that music. I drank it in.

And now, when I'm getting awfully close

to the other end, to the end,

when I hear those songs,

I feel a strange happiness.

And then there was

Otis

Redding.

When I started buying his records, with "Otis Blue,"

he already had two albums,

so I went out and got them too.

And I spent many hours listening

to that rough sweet voice.

"That's How Strong My Love Is."

I heard the Rolling Stones' version first.

and I liked it fine, more than fine,

when Mick Jagger sang it,

I wouldn't take anything away from him.

I guess there was an element

of theft in it, young white guys

having hits with black music—

but also praise, and there were benefits

both ways across the Atlantic.

It was quite a musical time.

Love songs.

"I've Been Loving You Too Long."

What did I know about love? Nothing,

except for longing, mostly physical.

I'd had one girlfriend. I was eighteen.

But that didn't stop me

from feeling those songs,

or from listening to them over and over

in my teen-age rooms

on the mono record player

I carried with me like a small suitcase

with my soul inside

from place to place.

The spare, sharp guitar notes of Steve Cropper.

The organ of Booker T.

Duck Dunn's bass. Al Jackson's drums.

(No finer example of positive interaction

between whites and blacks,

of excellent, tight collaboration,

to be found in American history maybe,

than Booker T. and the MGs.)

The crisp and moaning horns.

The crisp and moaning horns.

Perfect accompaniment for Otis's voice,

with a texture as rough as the bark

of a wild cherry tree. Rough,

but sweet as dark cherries.

Janis Joplin was a big fan.

"Otis is God," she would say.

Very likely she was high

on something beside music when she said it,

but I do know what she meant.

His fast songs were just as good as the ballads.

Aretha Franklin's "Respect"

is a wonderful thing, a masterpiece for sure.

But it was Otis who wrote it,

and his version is also wonderful,

driving along to the horns and the snare drum of joy.

And "Try a Little Tenderness," both slow and fast,

beginning in the pure syllables of tenderness,

singing about a woman's weariness,

then building to the full throttle

of Otis's ecstatic got-ta got-ta got-tas.

If you want a song to go to heaven to,

to lift you up gradually

and then carry you away,

that would be a good choice.

But, in a different sort of mood,

another good choice would be

the song he's probably most famous for —

"(Sitting on) The Dock of the Bay."

It's unique. He was trying something new.

Otis's big, rich voice, so quiet among

 a simplicity of guitar, bass, and drums,

and delicate horns coming in.

And the little bit of whistling he does at the end.

Even the sound of waves, and the cry of gulls,

all work so well.

The gulls were Otis's idea,

but he never got to hear

the finished version, with their cries.

Steve Cropper added those.

Three days after the song was recorded, Otis was gone.

Plane crash in foggy winter lake.

He was twenty-six.

("Sitting on) The Dock of the Bay"

is a short song. Simple lyrics.

Otis Redding's version of Ecclesiastes.

Whenever I hear it, I can't believe how beautiful it is,

so sad, so calm. That song rocks

like a boat,

and Otis's voice

rows us home.

ONE OF THE RONETTES HAS DIED

I imagine that tonight male poets about my age all over the country

are writing poems in memory of Estelle,

one of The Ronettes,

who died yesterday.

Actually, I did not know

that her name was Estelle until now,

reading her obituary in *The New York Times*.

The only Ronette whose name I knew was Ronnie.

The other two were the other Ronettes.

All three were dark-eyed

way too much eye-shadow

black-haired hair-piled-high

hair flowing down over shoulders

beautiful.

I saw them on television a few times.

And in person once.

That was something

I will never forget,

the way they danced and swayed

in blue satin

very short dresses

in the pagan temple

of the Brooklyn Fox Theater.

I bought their records,

listened to them over and over—

what better songs could there be

than "Be My Baby,"

"Baby I Love You,"

"The Best Part of Breaking Up,"

and "Walking in the Rain"?

The wall of sound, clattering with tambourines,

cascading drums, much echo—

an amazing sound, some kind of reverberating opera—

brainchild of Phil Spector,

who married Ronnie

and ultimately in various ways

did all The Ronettes harm.

"She was the quiet Ronette,

the one people called the prettiest,

the one who was content

to remain in the shadow

of her younger sister, Ronnie,

because even in the shadow

there's still some spotlight,"

the eloquent obituary says.

I hadn't known until today

how hard life was for Estelle

after The Ronettes broke up.

Mental illness, wandering the streets, out of it,

telling people she was singing tonight

but she didn't know where.

Sometimes homeless.

Too bad Mick Jagger or George Harrison,

both of whom she dated,

didn't set up a trust fund for her.

She did come into some money

from a Ronettes lawsuit against Phil Spector,

but that was much later.

And she was able to attend her Ronette induction

into the Rock & Roll Hall of Fame,

though she couldn't perform.

Friends helped fix her up,

and she looked quite beautiful again.

Keith Richards introduced her,

and she gave an acceptance speech,

which I will quote in full:

"I would just like to say

thank you very much

for giving me this award. I'm Estelle,

of The Ronettes. Thank you."

Does she belong in the Hall of Fame?

The back-up singer.

Wa-oo-oo-oo.

The swaying dancer.

Of course. How could you possibly exclude her?

I imagine that male poets about my age all over the country

are writing poems for her tonight.

GODZILLA

There's a re-make of *Godzilla* at the movies this summer,

so I took my eight-year-old grandson to see it.

"I really want to see it," he said.

We sat in the cool, almost empty matinee

and took it all in. The legendary monster.

The computer-generated movie spectacle.

He asked, during the long build-up,

when ominous signs were making it clear

that something was very wrong

in the nuclear power plants of Japan,

"Where's Godzilla?"

Eventually other monsters appeared,

creatures hard to tell whether giant insects or machines,

and after those had torn Japan apart for a while

and were headed for California,

then Godzilla appeared.

My grandson moved over from his seat

and sat in my lap for a while—

a sign that the movie must have been pretty good.

And it was. I won't tell you how it ended.

Afterward, he wanted to hear about the original.

I'd told him I saw when I was a kid, about his age.

He was deeply interested.

"How many monster movies did you see," he asked,

"when you were a kid?"

"Oh, I saw a lot of them.

Probably a hundred at least." Soon after that

I put the old *Godzilla* on my Netflix queue,

the American version, with footage of Raymond Burr

spliced in— the one I saw in 1956.

When it arrived we watched it together.

Once again, during the long build-up, he asked,

"Where's Godzilla?" and I said,

"Just wait—it won't be long now."

Through more than half a century I knew

exactly when Godzilla

would appear over the crest of a hill—

just briefly, a glimpse, but long enough to terrify the people

of the remote fishing village.

And I remembered how Godzilla

would look, that crazy toothy head.

And then, after more confusion, scientists

and military officials rushing around,

trying to figure out what was going on—

all hell broke loose. Godzilla

rose out of Tokyo Bay,

came lumbering out of the black water.

Tokyo was surrounded by high voltage power lines…

maybe they would stop him.

No—forget that.

Godzilla's fiery breath melted the towers

like candles hit by a blowtorch,

and as the wires crackled and sparked,

he strolled on through,

crushing railroad yards,

demolishing buildings with the sweeps of his tail.

(*His* tail? Was Godzilla male?

I didn't think about it

when I was a kid, but a friend of mine

who also remembers the film, and is a scientist,

says she always assumed that Godzilla was a female.)

Who could forget the newscaster in the tall building,

drenched with sweat, yelling into his microphone

as Godzilla came closer?

Who could forget

the spectacle of Godzilla

calmly destroying the city—

with an occasional magnificent roar,

with blasts of fire, back-plates incandescent,

in magnificent tableaus of chaos.

Primitive special effects?

A guy in a rubber suit

destroying models? I guess so.

But there was a certain undeniable

grandeur to the proceedings.

A Japanese city going up in black and white flames, in 1956.

Do you remember how they killed Godzilla?

A scientist who wore a black eye patch

had just invented a device

that took all the oxygen out of water.

There was a scary scene where he

takes his girlfriend into his lab

and gives her a demonstration.

It turned the fish in the aquarium into skeletons.

She screams and bursts into tears.

It was called, "The Oxygen Destroying Device."

He wanted to keep it a secret,

but now the girlfriend knew, and the secret got out.

And now there was also

Godzilla to deal with.

As another scientist, an older man, said,

"The future is unknown, but Godzilla is reality."

The ships went out. There was an air of hope,

Japanese military music playing.

Two men went down in diving suits,

the old fashioned kind, with round metal heads.

One of them was the scientist with the black eye patch.

Godzilla was down there, resting.

Tired after destroying Tokyo.

There were shots of Godzilla moving about

slowly in the ocean depths.

The oxygen destroying device was not large.

One man could carry it. After he'd set it off,

bubbling in the water,

the man with the eye patch

produced a knife from somewhere

in his diving suit, and cut his air hose.

He was hoping to take the secret

with him, because, as he had said,

"This device must never be used again."

So pretty soon, it only took moments,

Godzilla turned into a skeleton,

and the bones rolled over and sank to the bottom.

It was exactly as I remembered it.

As the credits were rolling, I asked my grandson,

"How did you like that?" "Good," he said.

He didn't say "awesome," but I think he did catch

some of the awesomeness of it,

because now and then he asks me, out of nowhere,

"Do you remember the oxygen destroying device?"

And I say, "Yes, I do."

And I remember Tokyo burning.

The grand ominous murky music.

Godzilla turning and going back again, unforgettable,

into the dark waters of the bay.

MONTE IRVIN HAS PASSED

I hear on the radio that he has died,

and I can immediately picture him.

A black face. Big smile. The Giants.

This comes from baseball cards.

For a few years, I knew the names

and the faces of all the major leaguers.

He was one of the first black players,

after Jackie Robinson broke the color line.

He was twenty-nine by then, old for a rookie—

"You should have seen me when I was nineteen,

when I could really play," he said.

He'd been a star in the Negro Leagues,

and he was still a formidable player

for a while in the majors. Hit with power.

Rifle arm in the outfield. Stole home in the World Series.

I think the only person I've known personally

who was named Monte

was one of the black kids in my class in school.

Monte Johnson. In my school in New Jersey,

there were three or four black kids

in a class of twenty-five. We got along fine,

as far as I knew, but we didn't socialize

outside of school. It would have been unusual

for me to go to their houses, or for them to come to mine.

The only trouble I can remember

was when Wesley Jenkins joined the Boy Scout troop

and one of the kids, our patrol leader, called him Satch.

Mrs. Jenkins came to the scout meeting one night,

I remember her coming in, and she and the scoutmaster

left the room. That took some courage.

Wesley dropped out of the troop soon after that.

I've wondered sometimes what happened to Wesley.

He was a big kid, the only one who could hit the ball

over the fence in Little League. And Monte,

and Phil Beamer, and Weldon and Walter Leach, twins,

and Ralph Alexander, and Carol and Gloria Daniels.

Like me, they're about to hit seventy.

I wonder how things went for them.

On the radio Willie Mays talked beautifully about Monte Irvin.

He said how much he helped him when he came up, what a good friend

he was, how he helped him avoid a lot of mistakes.

Even if you're Willie Mays, it's good to have Monte Irvin in the outfield beside you.

MEN'S CLOTHING STORE

I go in to buy a shirt for my son.

He's turning forty next week.

I look through the piles of shirts on the shelves,

in the cool of the air conditioning.

July. It's 95 degrees outside.

While I leaf through the shirts,

I have a conversation with Lenny.

I've been buying clothes from him

for nearly forty years. His father

owned the store before him, and his grandfather

before that. Lenny started working here

when he was a teen-ager,

and now he's close to 60.

The sign outside says, "Since 1917."

Here we are in 2014, so I ask him,

"Are you getting ready for the centennial?"

Yes, he is, he says, though he hasn't decided

what form the celebration will take.

100 years in the men's clothing business.

That's something. Spending your whole life

doing what your father did, and your grandfather,

and in the same location—that's something.

He tells me about when they expanded, 35 years ago—

knocked out a wall and took over the store next door,

where the suits and pants are now.

His father was running the place back then.

Business was good. They needed the space.

"Those were the days. The salad days.

We had seven people working here then!"

he says. That was before

the malls and the factory outlet stores

dropped like development bombs

out in the cornfields west of town.

Things are quieter now.

But he's got loyal customers,

and he does a good business in uniforms.

"Well, it's still a nice store," I say,

as he wraps up the bright but tasteful

red and blue plaid short-sleeve shirt that I've chosen.

Woolrich, made in Bangladesh.

First in a box, then in a sheet of dark green paper

he tears, with a satisfying, ripping sound,

along the old cast iron paper holder's long blade.

THE DIFFERENCE BETWEEN QUAKERISM
AND CATHOLICISM

There are quite a few actually, but here's one.

I've been going to mass a couple of times a week lately.

I take a friend who's in assisted living

and couldn't get there otherwise,

so I feel qualified to speak about this.

Well, not "feel qualified" exactly,

but I have noticed something.

I'm definitely not a Catholic,

and I don't consider myself exactly a Quaker either,

at any rate not a very good one, not the authentic article,

though I've been going to meeting

for almost forty years.

With Quakerism, with its periods of silence

and permission for anyone to speak—

anyone who feels moved by the spirit, or the Spirit—

and what that might mean is of course

open to individual interpretation,

and how high one's standards are

for inspiration—with Quakerism,

you might be surprised.

You never know what might be going on

out there in the world of inner light.

But with Catholicism,

you pretty much know what will happen.

The ritual is very much the same every day—

it's a ritual, after all— and not only that,

the content is printed out in a book,

that was of course prepared in advance

somewhere, I'm not sure where,

I'm guessing the Vatican.

In any case, spontaneity

is not the name of the game.

The priest's homily,

after the reading of the Gospel,

is the only place where individual

inspiration might come in,

and in the church I've been attending,

I haven't noticed much of that.

The priest is an old man, he walks with a cane,

and his messages are short

and amount to "be good," and "God loves us,"

and "we hope we go to heaven."

I'm simplifying somewhat, but not much.

So what I think is, the quality varies more

in Quakerism. I go to meeting every Sunday,

and it's partly out of curiosity,

to see who will speak, and what they'll say.

I've come out more than once

at the rise of meeting (as we say) thinking,

"Was that really worth listening to?"

I shouldn't judge. But so it goes.

And sometimes people, ordinary people,

who I know, say moving, insightful,

and quite wonderful things.

And then, of course, there's the silence,

sitting together in silence,

which can be very nice,

once you acquire a taste for it.

Sometimes a lovely sideways silence.

And there are weeks when no one

says anything for the whole hour,

and that can be the best of all.

Sit in silence, speak, don't speak.

Quakers tried to get rid of all rituals,

and what was left? A ritual!

But a rather spare one, and while a ritual,

you never know what someone might say.

On the other hand, in the mass,

they keep things moving along,

and there is a sameness that even I, a newcomer, an outsider, have started to find, in a way, reassuring—

predictable, a familiar beauty

in the motions, and an authentic humility

in going with the script, and not thinking

that what you think is so important, accepting instead

motions and words prepared by others—

almost every word prepared in advance,

and some a long time ago.

Both ways have their advantages, no doubt.

ERNIE BANKS AND BILL MONBOUQUETTE

"As you move on in your life, you come to think

you really don't have to win to win."

-Ernie Banks

A week or so ago, Ernie Banks died.

No doubt you remember him.

Great Cubs shortstop. Hit for power.

"Mr. Cub." Good-natured, easy-going.

One of his records: Not once ejected

in his career of 2,528 games.

"Let's play two" was his contribution

to the lexicon of memorable baseball sayings.

Since he played during the years

when I was collecting baseball cards,

I have a clear picture of him in my mind.

For whatever reason—homers, smile, Cubs blue?—

he was one of my favorite players,

even though I lived a thousand miles from Chicago.

You never know who you're going to find

looking out at you when you open to the *The New York Times*

obituary page. Last week, Ernie Banks, a few days later,

Bill Monbouquette. Red Sox pitcher. Same era.

Not one of the immortals (as we like to say).

A middle-echelon player—though in saying such a thing

we forget how far, how very far,

the middle echelon is above us.

Lifetime record: 114 wins, 112 losses.

It sounds mediocre. But anyone who wins

more than 100 games in the majors…

well, very few people could do it.

He had one no-hitter. The final batter

was Luis Aparicio, future Hall of Famer.

"It was August 1, 1962. I had Aparicio

0 and 2, and threw him a slider off the plate.

He tried to hold up, and I thought he went

all the way. The umpire, Bill McKinley,

called it a ball, and as I was getting the ball back

from the catcher, someone shouted from the stands,

'They shot the wrong McKinley.'

I had to back off the mound because

I had a little chuckle to myself.

The next pitch, I threw him another slider,

and he swung and missed.

They say white men can't jump, but I did.

It's about the biggest thrill I ever had."

These slippings away are so mysterious,
these reminders in the obituaries.
It feels a little different when it is one
of the greats who dies, Ernie Banks, say,
than when it is some lesser figure,
like Bill Monbouquette. A slightly
different tone, but the same mystery —
something I didn't know was in the cards
when I was sorting them, long ago.
I can picture their faces. Their names,
like poems. And now, today —
who could forget him? —
Orestes "Minnie" Minoso.

CLOSED RESTAURANT

One of my favorite restaurants has closed.

Bar on one side, not too much light,

but not too dark. Knotty pine from the old days.

And then a doorway through

to the other side, and the tables and booths.

White paper on the tables,

but at first you could take it for linen.

Not too noisy. Several kinds of beer on tap,

served in tall thick glasses.

My usual entrée: a personal pizza, 12 inches diameter,

vegetarian, mushrooms, olives, and green peppers.

Excellent chewy crust.

In this town of many pizzas,

theirs was one of the best.

But it wasn't a pizza place.

It was a nice restaurant, with tablecloths,

even if they were made of paper.

The servers were all female, pretty.

The women reading this may not care about pretty,

but don't blame me if they were pretty —

and it was definitely part of the ambience.

They told you the specials,

with just the right amount

of pretense to flatter us,

crusted this and drizzled that.

But really there was nothing

pretentious about the place,

and I was comfortable ordering my pizza,

and my cool tall glass of Labatt's.

Then suddenly, a sign on the door:

"Closed—thanks for your business!"

Later we heard it was because the owners,

a married couple, split up.

The restaurant seemed to be doing well,

but apparently not the couple.

Things are always falling apart

or breaking down somewhere. Have you noticed that?

There are other restaurants, but I particularly liked that one.

I'm just saying, enjoy your good meal,

the friendly service of your pretty waitress,

your tall glass of cold beer, or glass of wine,

your table or booth, while you've got them.

RATTLESNAKE

Driving along the gravel road through Loyalsock State Forest,

coming back from a hike to Angel Falls,

something in the road ahead.

Something long and straight.

A stick? No, not a stick. Approaching,

we see it is a snake, and stopping

a little ways before it, clearly it is

a rattlesnake. We pull up closer, a close rattlesnake

viewing, from the safety of the car.

Timber rattler. Dark, almost black.

Somewhere between three and four feet long.

A beauty of a rattlesnake—if beauty is the word

for a rattlesnake. I have an impulse

to get out of the car and urge it onward,

but my wife says, No,

and of course she's right,

why tempt fate, and another car

might not pass here for hours.

So we sit and watch, and now the snake

has noticed that something is going on.

What does the snake brain make

of the large object looming nearby?

Picked up by tongue? Snakes don't have ears,

but they hear vibrations in the bones of their jaws,

I'm told. We've got the windows open. We're talking,

making perceptive comments like,

"Wow, look at it!" And now it is not

stretched out straight, and it has stopped

its forward progress, gone into a semi-coil.

It is looking back over its shoulder

which it doesn't have,

looking up toward us, its triangular head rising

six inches off the ground.

It does not go so far as to rattle.

It reassesses, it eases, and turns again,

continues its slow slither

to the edge of the road, and then off into the rocks

and the mountain laurel bushes.

Majestically, might be the word for it.

When I get home, I do a little research.

I shouldn't be surprised,

but there are dozens of YouTube videos of rattlesnakes—

apparently a whole sub-culture

of rattlesnake aficionados.

People in shorts and boots.

Some harass them.

They like to hear the rattler's buzz,

and you can't really blame them.

It is a thrilling sound.

Others are scientists, taking a census,

taking measurements, before they release them.

Some are just hikers,

carrying their phones with them of course,

so they stop and record a minute or two

of rattlesnake encounter,

minimal drama, no meaning,

just the rattlesnake

on the trail, and its slow withdrawing.

Legless terrestrial, hearing with its bones,

sampling the air

with flickering forked tongue.

What does it see

through the slits of its eyes?

Its slow cruising through eternity.

Slithering slowly. Gliding—

majestically, might be the word for it.

I'm not sure what the word for it is.

MONSTERS

I'm here to say a few words
in praise of the savage wonder
of the old horror movies.
At this point, a lot of horror movies are old.
I don't mean the oldest, the silents,
some of which were very good,
"The Phantom of the Opera," for example,
and deserve their own poem.

But just after that, in the 1930s,
when the movies had just learned to speak,
there was a look, a feel,
some black and white purity,
and a new…you wouldn't want to call it
sophistication perhaps, but
something primitive in their modernity.
For whatever reasons, including
what the zeitgeist, the events of the thirties,
may have contributed,
the horror movies were in some kind
of glorious period of greatness.
Images right out of the collective unconscious.
"Dracula," with Bela Lugosi.

"Frankenstein," with Boris Karloff.

It doesn't get any better than that.

Those are the most famous ones.

But there was also "The Invisible Man."

There was also, "WereWolf of London."

"The Old Dark House," with Boris Karloff.

"The Mummy," with Boris Karloff.

I hadn't seen that one for a long time,

and I remembered it as slow-moving

from when I saw it on TV when I was a kid

lying on the living room floor late at night.

But I remembered the opening scene,

and when I went to YouTube and watched it again,

I could see why I remembered it.

It's where the mummy comes to life,

and yes it was slow-moving—

the slowness of someone 3000 years old.

But not boring. Anything but boring.

The oblivious archeologist is sitting in the tomb

poring over the sacred scrolls,

and right behind him, in his upright casket

where they've leaned it against the wall,

the mummy

is coming to life.

Silently, slowly,

the opening of an eye,

the hands moving

in their ragged wrappings.

And then switch back to the archeologist

intent on the scrolls,

and when the mummy's hand

appears on the table beside him,

the archeologist looks up

at who is standing there beside him

and he goes absolutely raving mad.

And when the mummy has gone away

taking the scroll and dragging his rags behind him,

and when his colleague rushes in ,

the archeologist is laughing hysterically, and he says,

"He went for a little walk!"

The bad kind of resurrection.

Well, it's quite terrific.

"The Raven," with Karloff and Lugosi.

"The Black Cat," with Karloff and Lugosi.

"Island of Lost Souls" was wild,

with Charles Laughton, and Lugosi.

Everyone knows Laughton was a great actor,

but so was Lugosi—the marvelous, outrageous

Bela Lugosi.

"The Bride of Frankenstein" was a beautiful film.

I have a picture of them hanging on my wall right now,

the awkward, hopeful monster

holding his bride's hand.

And there was the one in which the monsters

were not monsters at all, but people

with physical deformities, living in a sideshow,

and in the crudeness of the time,

it was called "Freaks." It had a horrifying ending

that involved crawling through the mud

in pouring rain at night.

I won't try to describe it.

If you want to know what happened,

you'll have to check it out for yourself.

And in those same few years,

"King Kong," for God's sake,

with as much excitement and profound symbolism

as it is possible for one movie to have.

Sometimes I think it contains the whole 20th century.

Nature, sex, race, capitalism, commercialism,

urbanization, technology….

Remember the gas bombs?

Remember Kong ripping apart the el,

the drowsy commuters, not knowing what awaited them,

coming oblivious down the track?

And the fucking airplanes, buzzing

around the Empire State Building—

do I need to say anything about that?

All that the later versions can do is pay homage.

Computer generated special effects,

adding a couple more Tyrannosaurus Rexes

for Kong to battle, can do nothing to improve it.

Laughton's "Hunchback of Notre Dame"

came in just as the decade was ending.

Not a horror movie, a giant spectacle, big crowd scenes—

but somehow he belongs with the others, the hunchback,

though he was not a monster,

but the sweetest, saddest man.

But if you want to talk about frightening,

perhaps the greatest of all

is "Dr. Jekyll and Mr. Hyde" (1932).

It wasn't the first, and it wasn't the last,

but something about this version

sets it apart. Robert Louis Stevenson

had a great idea, and this movie distilled it,

perverse and perfect.

Rouben Mamoulian

was the director.

He knew what he was doing.

Or maybe he didn't.

For all the artistic touches,

watching it you might wonder

if he was operating on instinct.

Fredric March

got into it.

The Oscars were a new thing back then.

They gave him the Oscar for Best Actor.

He deserved it.

With the help of the make-up department

and the still young magic of cinema,

transformations of creature into creature

were more vivid than ever before possible.

March turned himself into something, into someone,

you would never want to meet —

but when Mr. Hyde first appears, looking in a mirror,

you shudder with fascination

at his toothy, liberated glee.

He twitches with surprise and happiness.

The first time he ventures out into the city,

it's pouring rain, and he looks up,

his eyes flashing and blinking into the rain.

It's when he goes to the dance hall

that things go bad. An ape-like man

in gentleman's clothes,

he sits at his private table.

He looks out, delighted, at the drinking,

the carousing, the dancing girls.

I don't like comparing him to an ape.

It's not fair to apes.

When the waiter waits too long for a tip,

he grabs the bottle by its neck

and smashes it against the table,

and you can see perfectly clearly

that he would have no problem using it on the waiter.

He tells him to send over

the saloon girl who's caught his eye.

He remembers her

from when he treated her when he was Dr. Jekyll.

Her name is Ivy. She's played by Miriam Hopkins,

in one of the sexiest performances ever committed to film.

She flirted with Jekyll, pretending to be injured.

She slipped off her garters. She undid her dress.

Naked under the sheet, she dangled her leg

over the edge of the bed.

She almost seduced the handsome doctor. It was very close.

But now he has come back to her

as Mr. Hyde.

She's startled by his ugliness, but she pulls herself together.

She thinks she's tough enough to handle him.

But she isn't.

The scenes between her and Hyde are the really scary ones.

He sets her up in a nice apartment.

He keeps her there. She can't leave

for terror of what he'll do if she tries.

A hideous creep has her where he wants her.

He comes and goes as he pleases.

At one point Jekyll vows to give it up, to go straight,

never to drink the potion again.

But he's drunk it too many times,

and walking through the park one evening

on his way to a dinner party,

he finds himself turning into Hyde again—

the hairy, darkening hands at his cuffs,

the elongated, protruding teeth filling his mouth.

Ivy thinks that Hyde is gone, and won't be back.

She's having a glass of champagne

by herself in the apartment,

toasting her deliverance, her salvation.

Mamoulian places her

where we can see the landing, the door

in the background behind her.

And the door slowly opens.

Hyde quietly enters.

We see him before she does.

Be aware, whoever you are, reading this,

that my movie recommendations don't always work out.

Many times, friends have wondered

what I was thinking when I picked the movie.

But in this case, the critics tend to agree with me.

One calls it "a hallucinatory, feverish classic."

I used it in a class once, Film & Literature.

"Dr. Jekyll and Mr. Hyde" —a natural.

But when I showed it, one woman,

an older woman, retired, unmarried,

dropped the course.

I enjoyed having her in class.

She had more energy than the twenty-year-olds.

She said interesting and insightful things.

When she told me she was dropping, I urged her to stay.

But no, she'd decided to drop the class,

she didn't really want to explain.

I felt bad about it.   I didn't mean to offend.

I was trying to put together a good course.

Stimulating. Works of art people should know.

I don't have a lot of regrets

from a long career in teaching,

but I still feel a little bad about that.

I hope you find all this interesting.

I read the above the other day to my wife and a friend,

we were sitting out on the patio, sipping iced tea,

and their lack of fascination was pretty apparent.

In my wife's eyes I saw,

"Hmm, so this is what he's been doing

at the desk all morning."

My friend was polite. He said it was "vivid."

But I could tell, not as vivid

as these films are to me.

So I've decided to set it aside.

If I ever run into Frederic March,

I'd like to read it to him.

Or Rouben Mamoulian.

Maybe they would enjoy it.

Or Miriam Hopkins—in my dreams .

As for Mr. Hyde, I don't think I'd read it to him.

He didn't have the slightest interest in poetry.

He'd just as soon hit me with a bottle. If he was your son,

and it was time for him to go off to college,

you'd worry. You'd hope he gets his act together.

You'd hope for the best.

ZOO

It is a beautiful day for the zoo. May.

The sun shining. Warm, but still cool.

Lots of people out, enjoying the day at the zoo.

Families, strolling around. The South African penguins

look content, a big troop of them standing

on the little concrete ledge, individuals

slipping in and out of the pool.

And then, the polar bear. We are lucky enough

to catch her taking a swim. Behind the glass,

she's doing water ballet, white fur flowing

as she dives to the bottom, where she bats at a blue ball.

So easy in the water. Now she does a back flip!

And when she climbs out, we can see her above us,

through the glass and water, shaking herself off,

like a dog does—but this is not a dog,

it's a polar bear! And we are watching her. Wonderful.

The Baltimore zoo has a black rhino,

and he's not just lazing around today.

He has a reasonable yard, well, it's bigger than a pen,

and there's a nice mud wallow

which right now he is enjoying, lying on his side, rolling

almost up onto his back at times, lolling his massive head

into the puddle. We take it for granted

from having seen them in books all our lives,

those horns on the snout,

but though this is not my first rhino

and I've recently turned 70,

it has never quite hit me before

how incredible a rhino's body is.

An NFL player is slight

compared to the powerful thickness and tapering of it.

At least we have a good word

for this magnificent creature:

rhinoceros.

Luckily, nobody has trimmed or removed his horn.

When he decides he's done with the mud bath,

he gets up, half his body darkened,

and heads off at a gait both massive and delicate.

The rhino trot.

And so it goes. The lemurs haunt

their tree-filled cage. The tortoises, ranging in size

from bowling ball to riding lawn mower,

move around their yard

with exquisite slowness. Maybe no other creature

inhabits the stillness as deeply as they do.

The giraffes, huge elongated antelopes,

can't go far, no flowing across the savannah,

but they manage still to be graceful

in the sway of their motions.

And now the elephants, four of them,

two females on one side, an enormous bull on the other,

a younger male in a third pen behind the house.

He can't be in the same enclosure with his mother,

nor with the mature bull.

It is always an honor

to see an elephant in person.

A keeper is in the yard with the females, giving a pedicure.

The bigger female raises her great round foot

and folds it under, and rests it on a stool.

Her toenails do not wear down as they would

if she were walking great distances.

Meanwhile, the bull has let down his cock,

longer than a golf bag, and much more limber.

It hangs there, swaying slightly.

After a while, he pulls it back up,

or it pulls itself back up.

Don't know what was going on with that.

Normal ebb and flow, I suppose.

I doubt it was display—but who knows?

It's an interesting and pleasant day at the zoo.

Now we come to the chimpanzees.

They have an enclosure about the size of an elementary school gym,

the terrain is sloped, and trunks and limbs cut from dead trees

angle and corkscrew the space.

Some rudimentary gym equipment. Some shelves for lounging.

It's a troop of about twenty. Enough for a community —

to have multiple relationships, to keep each other company,

opportunities for mutual grooming.

But what I'm seeing doesn't look like equanimity.

Everybody looks pensive, maybe depressed.

It's clear they're having thoughts, but not what they are.

I wonder if this is the mood

of a chimpanzee group in the wild.

Certainly they don't seem to be interested

in interacting with us, who stand on the other side

of the glass. Nowhere near as interested

as we are in looking at them. We, of course,

can walk away when we've looked enough.

There are twenty-five or thirty of us.

Only two of them are front and center, near the glass.

One is sitting on a branch, facing the other way.

Another is squatting directly in front of us,

and he is looking at us.

His expression could be human,

except that he's not human.

Inscrutable, but not daydreaming.

I would say, thoughtful, focused.

I stand for several minutes,

taking it all in, fascinated

by how much they look like us,

and how much they don't.

My attention comes back

to the one in front, and just then,

he explodes. He flips the plastic tub

beside him into the air, he vaults himself

crashing into and across the glass, and he shrieks,

and we all jump back and exclaim, whoa!,

as he retreats in two almost instantaneous leaps

to the rear of the enclosure, where he hunches

and looks back over his shoulder,

with an expression that I swear says,

"What do you think of that, motherfuckers?"

I guess you might translate

the whole performance in different ways,

but one would have to be

that the zoo is a wonderful place

except for the captivity,

if you are a being

who cares about privacy.

How different is it

from putting humans on display? Good question.

The zoo is a wonderful place.

SUPERMARKET

I go to the supermarket almost every day.

It's not that I need so many groceries.

I walk around with one of those little plastic baskets

they have for small orders. I think of this and that.

I can always use another box of shredded wheat.

And I always buy *The New York Times*,

which always has plenty of bad news,

and a picture, usually grim, on the front page.

But the supermarket is where I go

to relax, to unwind at the end of the day.

Very often, it's almost comical how often,

I meet a retired guy I know,

and sometimes I almost say,

"Dave, what are you doing here again? Get a life!"

But I don't. We don't know each other

that well. I just nod and say hello, raising my hand

in the ancient carrying-no-weapons gesture.

No doubt he's practicing, in his own way,

the same relaxation technique that I am.

Drifting along the aisles

is a way of taking in a certain calm,

to watch the world going about

some of its simpler business.

And it's a way of connecting with,

or at least being among, the human race.

Something healthy and ordinary

in people doing a daily errand,

buying groceries. But at the same time,

in their bodies, in their faces,

so many of them are wearing

marks of weakness, marks of woe.

That last line I borrowed

from my friend Bill Blake.

The supermarket where I go

has some amenities— not like the A&P

I knew when I was a kid.

For example, rest rooms.

A natural foods section,

with fifty kinds of herbal teas,

crackers and chips made from grain

that has not been genetically modified.

Almost half the produce section is organic.

Just today I bought a bag

of three Organic Romaine Hearts.

All of this is good. You might call it progress.

Another amenity is Café Square,

where you can sit and eat a sub

or a slice of pizza, or have a cup of coffee.

You can even just sit there,

not eating anything, with someone or alone,

out of the summer heat, out of the winter cold.

The people who congregate there

tend to be a segment of the population

with plenty of marks of weakness, marks of woe.

They have a sort of looped

and windowed raggedness.

There are small cohorts of geezers,

talking about the things geezers discuss.

Also couples, sometimes talking,

sometimes not. Also some solitaries.

I'm pretty sure some of the people

are mentally ill, spending their day alone.

In fact, I know some of them are.

It tends to be a shabby bunch.

Some are in sweat pants, or are they pajamas?

It makes a casual ambience,

but as I say, plenty of marks

of weakness, marks of woe.

Bill has a way of saying things.

One day, as we were sitting in Café Square,

he said, "To generalize is to be an idiot,"

but five minutes later he said,

"Man was made for joy and woe,

and when this we rightly know,

through the world we safely go,"

which is a kind of generalization.

He's an optimist, but of a complicated sort.

After pausing for a moment, he went on,

"Joy and woe are woven fine,

a clothing for the soul divine." I don't know

if the people in the supermarket

know that. Maybe they do.

I'm not even sure if it's true.

Clothing for the soul divine? It might be.

But marks of weakness, marks of woe—

that's definitely true. Joy and woe.

He has a way of thinking in opposites.

Innocence and experience;

eternity and the productions of time—

he weaves them together,

they're always slinging themselves

into each other when he talks. It's a rare gift.

And somehow he manages to say things like that

without being obnoxious or preachy.

Another good one is about the trick

of living in the moment.

We all know that it's not as easy as it ought to be.

But Bill says, "He who binds to himself a joy,

does the winged life destroy.

But he who kisses the joy as it flies

lives in eternity's sunrise."

You see what I mean?

It's perfect. You just have to be careful,

when kissing the joy

that you don't throw your neck out.

Once when we were sitting

with our slices of pizza, a fly

was buzzing around him.

He flicked it away, but didn't swat it.

And he said, "Am not I a fly like thee?

Or are you not a man like me?

For I dance and drink and sing,

Till some blind hand

Shall brush my wing."

So simple. But it's about the best thing

I ever heard anyone say about mortality.

So when I meet someone I know in the supermarket,

which I almost always do, it's a small city,

I try to keep Bill's words in mind.

I smile, nod, say hello. Sometimes

we have a little conversation.

With strangers, you have to be careful

about eye contact, you shouldn't overdo it.

But even with the strangers

I sometimes nod and smile—

not mentioning of course

the marks of weakness, marks of woe,

as on our separate ways we go.

MUDDY WATERS HOWLIN' WOLF
BO DIDDLEY CHUCK BERRY

Well, Phil Chess has died, at 95,

who with his brother Leonard

started a record company, Chess Records,

and they recorded a truly amazing

group of musicians. It's nice the way

fate works things out sometimes,

the connections, the incongruities—

two sons of Polish immigrants being the ones

to record, in the unique bare bones acoustics

of their studio, and to present to the world,

the great blues sounds, and then some,

of Muddy Waters, Howlin' Wolf, Bo Diddley, Chuck Berry.

Muddy Waters had the voice

of power, of authority, of glory,

the deep-down voice,

surrounded by the piercing notes

of his electric guitar. No wonder people knew

they were hearing something old and new

when they first heard him do

"I Can't Be Satisfied," "Baby Please Don't Go,"

and "Hoochie Coochie Man."

I saw him play once. He was older.

He sat in a chair with his guitar.

He let a younger guy do the flashy playing,

but he still had his mojo working,

his voice was still an exquisite, almost courtly

earthquake.

Muddy Waters Howlin' Wolf Bo Diddley Chuck Berry

Howlin' Wolf's voice was rougher,

but no less powerful. He was a big man,

maybe six foot six, and heavy-set.

He played the smallest instrument,

but when he took it out of his pocket,

the harmonica was not small,

its wailing and moaning alternating

with the rough thunder

of his voice singing the verses.

I saw him once in a small club in Greenwich Village.

He was wearing a baggy brown business suit,

and a skinny necktie. He had a great writhing

awkward sort of way

of dancing in his bigness,

and sometimes he jumped straight up and down,

like an earth-bound big-boned rocket.

At one point, in mid-song,

he lay down on the stage and rolled around,

and rumbled into the mic,

"I'm sorry, New York City,

I just can't help myself."

And then got up and went back to singing

"Smokestack Lightning."

Muddy Waters Howlin' Wolf Bo Diddley Chuck Berry

Bo Diddley had a song

called "Bo Diddley."

Once you've heard it, you never forget it.

That hand-jive rhythm will keep you alive

for years to come. He had a rectangular guitar.

He had another that was somewhere between

a lightning bolt and a star.

He wore black-rimmed glasses.

He had tall, glossy hair

(until in later years he started wearing a fedora,

that sported a silver-winged medallion).

He was as cool as cool could be,

it seemed to me. He had a song called

"I'm a Man." He had another

called "Dearest Darling,"

and another called "Pretty Thing"

(written by Willie Dixon).

I guess the only word for them

is primal. And another called "Mona."

Listening to that song, I wished

I knew Mona. Even today, I'd like to meet

Mona, at least in my dreams.

I saw him once in a small club in Greenwich Village.

He was fantastic. He was Bo Diddley,

in person, and eventually he played,

 "Bo Diddley." As I remember it

(I was eighteen or nineteen)

the place was riding along in spasms,

the air was quavering

to his shimmering guitar,

to the Bo Diddley beat.

Muddy Waters Howlin' Wolf Bo Diddley Chuck Berry

Chuck Berry wasn't like anybody else,

but he inspired everybody who came after.

As John Lennon said, if we needed another name

for rock and roll, it would be Chuck Berry.

And for all the influence, still nobody else sounds like him.

A few years, a string of hits—like flies caught in amber?

No way, they are not stuck. When you hear them now,

fifty, sixty years later, they are

just as fresh and alive as ever.

Still unique, thumping, jangling, and precise.

A certain beautiful spareness. I wonder

how many times he's played

"Roll Over Beethoven,"

"Nadine," and "Johnny B. Goode."

He was a brown-eyed handsome man—

also, as he originally wrote the line,

a brown-skinned handsome man,

but he changed it so as not

to alienate white record buyers.

Such, such were the times.

Either way, he was a poet,

his lyrics so tight, so vivid.

Check out "No Particular Place to Go"

or "Too Much Monkey Business," for example.

Lines William Blake might have written,

if he'd lived in the 20th century.

Now the news that he's got

a new album coming out,

of all new material. He's ninety.

I wonder what that will be like—Chuck Berry at ninety.

And me a teenager, plus fifty.

I think I'd better get that one.

I can't get certain geniuses out of my mind,

conscious or unconscious. Virtuoso

original interpreters of a great tradition.

Can't get them out of my system.

Why would I want to? They *are* my system.

Muddy Waters Howlin' Wolf Bo Diddley Chuck Berry

SISTER ROSETTA THARPE

Glad to hear that Sister Rosetta Tharpe has been elected

to the Rock & Roll Hall of Fame.

It's a nice recognition to have—

even though she's not here to enjoy it,

at least not able to attend

the ceremony in person.

Nina Simone got in too.

I never thought of her as a rock & roller,

but definitions are problematical.

Glad to have her in there too.

Sister Rosetta Tharpe, I knew about somewhat,

but when she got elected I went over to YouTube,

where you can see just about anything

you might want to see, or so it seems.

If you type in, say, Robert Burns,

hoping to see him reciting in some Scottish tavern,

you won't find him, though you will find

plenty of people reading and singing his poems.

But Sister Rosetta Tharpe—my God, there she is,

playing her guitar, singing and swaying,

picking and strutting, eyes flashing. That is joy.

Her stage presence, her style of singing—

visceral, theatrical, blues, gospel, wonderful.

Check out the one where she is playing

at a train station, in England, 1964.

She arrives in a horse-drawn carriage.

She climbs down, wearing a long white coat

and high-heel shoes, helped down by

a handsome young escort on her arm. She is about fifty.

They stroll along. She carries a huge gift

buoyantly down the platform.

When she comes to where the piano player

and the drummer and the stand-up bass player

are waiting, her guitar is waiting too, leaning,

and she picks it up and begins to play.

The crowd of kids on the other side of the track

are already clapping. She plays "Didn't It Rain."

Then she slows it down, for "Trouble in Mind."

At one point after a riff she interjects,

" Not bad for a woman, ain't it?" —

entirely secure in her prowess.

In some of her solos you can hear

Jimi Hendrix getting ready to be born.

I'd like to recommend a few other songs as well:

"This Train," "That's All,"

"Up above My Head," and of course

"Down by the Riverside."

Sister Rosetta Tharpe is in the Hall of Fame,

not just the one in Cleveland, nice as the honor may be,

but the real one, the big beautiful crumbling one

made of music and time.

LONG TERM CARE INSURANCE

People tell us it's good to have,

so we put in our application.

I don't feel quite right about it—

it feels a little selfish, too much concern

about myself, definitely not a lily of the fields

thing to do. Would Jesus

have long term care insurance?

As it turned out, he did not need it.

It would have been a dumb move for him.

Would Thoreau? No—

but he had his mother and sister

to take care of him, and they did a good job,

as he slowly died of tuberculosis.

At the end, when he couldn't manage stairs,

they moved his bed into the parlor—

the same small cane bed

he slept in at the cabin at Walden Pond.

But my friend, after his massive stroke,

told me in the nursing home, a pretty nice place

as nursing homes go, that he had

long term care insurance, and through

his half-paralyzed face he said,

"Best decision I ever made." So,

the nurse came to the house.

She works for John Hancock.

She had a few questions she wanted to ask us,

a few medical measurements, blood pressure,

blood sample, height and weight,

urine sample. She was checking us out.

The main part—I had a feeling

all the rest was just added on

to distract us from the real reason

for coming to see us in person—

was to test our mental functioning.

Alzheimer's. That's the big one.

My wife went first. One of us is going to go first—

but that's a different question. I mean,

my wife did the interview before me.

I went out and did some weeding in the garden.

After a while, my wife stuck her head

out the door and said, "Your turn."

I sat down, and we got started.

I seemed to know what day it was,

and what state I was in—that is,

New York. I think my answers

to the situational questions

were quite good. "If the bathtub

was overflowing, what would you do?"

"Turn off the water," I said.

"If you were home alone

and had swallowed poison,

what would you do? I assumed

she meant unintentionally, so I said,

"Call the poison control center

and ask what to do." Maybe "Call 911"

would have been a better answer,

certainly quicker than trying to find

the number of the poison control center,

but that was what I said.

I think I got all the math problems right—

except one, "What's 34 minus 9?"

I calculated, I said, "26"—

but caught myself, "No,

that's not right, it's 25."

I don't know if I was quick enough

to get credit for that one.

Repeating series of numbers went OK.

"4376"—""4376."

"52031"—"52031."

I was hoping it wouldn't go on too much longer,

the numbers stretching out,

but luckily she stopped at six digits.

Right at the beginning, she gave me a list of ten words,

and I enjoyed that, making up sentences,

for simple words— "maple," "road," "baseball."

"Willie Mays was a great baseball player."

I happened to be reading his biography.

And I thought to myself, "Nice sentence.

Simple. Specific. Not to mention, true."

The nurse did not comment on it,

or on any of my answers.

She was neutral, business-like.

Then, at the end of all the cognitive

questions, twenty minutes later,

as I thought she might,

she asked me to repeat

the ten words. I got quickly to seven,

no problem, but then, a cognitive

blank. I thought and thought,

while the nurse looked at me calmly.

Finally I came up with another: "sofa."

I asked if there was a time limit.

"No," she said. "Take your time."

The quiet in the room was profound.

Finally, another came to me: "truck."

But I never could get #10,

so, embarrassed, I conceded defeat.

She wasn't going to tell me

what the tenth word was, so I asked her.

"Cloud," she said.

Then we went on to the physical.

She took my blood pressure.

She jabbed my arm for blood.

Took blood pressure again.

She took out a scale

that looked like a laptop computer,

and I stepped onto it.

I weighed a little more than I expected,

but not too bad. Finally,

I went into the bathroom

with the little cup she gave me.

My cup did not run over.

Not sure whether half empty or half full.

No, definitely half full.

The worst part about it was when,

between blood pressure #2 and 3,

she measured my height, and said,

"Five feet nine inches." I said,

"Really? I think I'm five ten."

"Do you want me to measure you again?"

she asked. "Well, yes," I said.

She measured me again.

"Five feet nine inches," she said.

"Gravity is having its way with you."

She said it pleasantly, matter-of-fact.

Of course, it doesn't mean anything to her.

But to me, it was a shock—

this first knowledge that

I have now, officially, started to shrink.

And we all know where that leads.

But—no problem. No problem!

This is what is supposed to happen.

It happened to my grandfather,

a stalwart man if there ever was one—

I remember him, on his way to 95,

getting smaller, right before my eyes.

My father—he didn't live long enough.

I don't think he got any smaller.

I saw *The Incredible Shrinking Man*

in 1957, and I remember it well.

I suppose there might be a giant spider

I will need to fight before I walk out

through the cellar window screen

into the starry night.

Willie Mays was a great baseball player.

I enjoy sitting on the sofa

reading the newspaper in the evening.

I am driving my truck down a road of clouds.

INSOMNIA

I have tried to tell myself

that I am sitting at the cave mouth,

near the campfire under the stars,

as the anthropologists of sleep

say people have always done.

Someone needs to stay awake,

keeping an ear out for an enemy

or thief, or dangerous animal,

moving quietly closer in.

Sometimes I try to make it a meditation.

"Peace and compassion to all sentient beings,"

I say. I can keep going with that a long time—

sometimes half the night.

I chant that one sometimes during the day as well.

Sometimes I say, "Lord Jesus Christ,

have mercy upon me, a sinner."

It was recommended to me,

not by a friend or counselor, it was

a Russian Orthodox priest actually,

and when I said that I am not exactly

a Christian, he said, "That's OK. Use it

anyway. It might do you some good."

Sometimes I try to use the time for planning.

Sometimes I count my blessings.

Thanks for friends, for example, the honor

and pleasure of having such earthly company.

I could get up and read. Sometimes I do.

But mostly I stay in the bed,

because it's comfortable there, it's warm—

there's another person, a woman,

and it is pleasant to lie there with her.

And there's always the hope

that pretty soon I'll fall asleep—

the moment when someone

in the dark chemicals of my brain

decides to flip the liquid switch—

a moment I can never remember.

But usually that moment is slow in coming,

it takes an hour or two, or three,

and sometimes it does not come at all

before the light comes leaking

slowly into the darkness.

Peace and compassion to all sentient beings.

Mostly what I do is worry,

my mind full of adrenaline.

I wish I could get it flowing as well during the day

Actually, it's not adrenaline I need

so much as calm and clarity.

I lie awake worrying

about the melting ice caps,

the diminishing glaciers, the tar-sands of Canada,

the fracking fields of Ohio and Pennsylvania,

North Dakota's ruined prairie,

the dams of China, India's intention

to go full speed ahead with coal,

gouge it from the earth for its billion people to burn

just as Europeans and Americans

burned it before them.

People I know are very concerned

about climate change, they rail against it,

and the next thing you know,

they're getting on an airplane

to fly across a continent or an ocean for a vacation!

They come back and say what a great trip it was!

I guess they have an exemption.

I've done it a few times myself.

I worry about people I love.

I worry about people unhappy in their marriages.

I worry about people whose marriages

have broken apart in misery.

I worry about responsibilities

I have undertaken that I do not think

I will be able to fulfill.

I worry about my friend who is mentally ill.

And further down the list, there's the worry

about the judgment of God.

It doesn't really make sense to me that God,

if God is anything like what those

who seem to know claim,

would punish God's poor

imperfect struggling creatures

beyond the suffering and confusion of this world.

Yet both Jesus and Muhammad, the heavy hitters

of the world's two largest religions,

our mainlines to divinity,

seem to take the idea quite seriously,

for all their talk of mercy.

I wouldn't call myself an atheist,

but sometimes when someone

acknowledges being one,

I feel a sensation as if someone

had made a simple honest statement

in a conversation where no one else quite is.

It could be, don't you think,

that we're on our own, and God,

whatever else God may be,

is as unconcerned about us as the stars.

There are the stars again.

Peace and compassion to all sentient beings.

So, maybe the thing to do is just accept

the hours of lying awake.

What good does my vigil do?

As far as I know, I have not chased off a single wolf.

Farther down the list is the thought:

What if there's insomnia in the afterlife?

Insomnia in eternity, which of course

could easily turn into an eternity of insomnia....

I was hoping for a good night's sleep.

WHOSE BIRTHDAY IS IT TODAY?

I pay attention

to whose birthday it is today.

For me, it's a ritual—

rarely do I miss a day.

There's this radio show, 5 minutes long,

that every day tells you

who was born on this day, and in what year.

It's called "The Writer's Almanac,"

so the names are skewed toward writers,

but all sorts of artists

and historically important

and culturally interesting people

are included as well.

Events too. For example, today was the day

when the first atomic bomb

was successfully tested, or

Yosemite National Park was established.

At the end, a poem is read,

which is sometimes the best part, sometimes not.

That's how it is with poetry—

sometimes it's the best part,

sometimes not.

But it's the birthdays I wanted to talk about.

I don't know why exactly, but I find it

so interesting to know these things

at the beginning of the day—

who was born, what happened,

and sometimes, when it is suddenly

the occasion to think of, say,

Herman Melville, or Vincent Van Gogh,

the name gives me a shot of adrenaline

and I guess I could call it, hope.

Melville. Van Gogh. Hope?

It certainly isn't their biographies.

It's words and paint.

And yet the biographies contain

the words and paint....

And then there are the combinations, the juxtapositions,

the coincidental tag-teams

of shared birthdays. For example,

did you know that Confucius and Ed Sullivan share a birthday?

2,500 years apart, but the same day of the earth's

swing around the sun.

And now that they've been mentioned together,

I notice that they look alike—

the statue of Confucius in my garden—

I knew he resembled somebody, and now I recognize

that it is Ed Sullivan—

the expression, the posture, the way they both

hold their hands together in front of them.

And then I compare their wisdom, which they both had,

though neither of them was perfect.

Part of Confucius's wisdom was just that, knowing

he wasn't, and never would be,

perfect. Ed's was for putting on

a good, wildly eclectic show—

"Open big, have a good comedy act,

put in something for children,

and keep the show clean," he said.

Which he did every week,

and along the way helped bring Elvis Presley,

The Beatles, and James Brown

into the American soul. Wisdom.

Today (October 2) was a great day for juxtapositions:

Groucho Marx and Wallace Stevens,

Nat Turner and Gandhi.

What does this tell you

about the validity of astrology?

The length of the thumbnail bios varies,

not by importance

but apparently by whim.

For Groucho, very little detail

about his life, but instead

we get some of his one-liners:

"Marriage is a wonderful institution.

That is, if you like living in an institution."

"I have nothing but confidence in you,

and very little of that."

"I don't care to belong to a club

that accepts people like me as members."

I'd heard them all before, but still

such perfect expression

is worth revisiting.

Then we move directly

to Nat Turner, who as we know

led a slave rebellion

in which between 55 and 65 white people were killed.

I knew that, but I hadn't known

that "at his trial he admitted

to leading the rebellion, but pleaded 'not guilty.'"

He was executed on November 11.

Then comes Wallace Stevens,

who is perhaps the least famous

of the four to many people,

but not to us literary listeners.

"You are in the presence

of one of the greatest minds of the 20th century,"

I remember my professor saying.

"The Emperor of Ice Cream."

"Thirteen Ways of Looking at a Blackbird."

"The House Was Quiet and the Night was Calm."

The insurance man

who walked to work.

Who never ate lunch

except for once a week

to break the monotony.

Wallace Stevens, who said,

"After one has abandoned a belief in god,

poetry is that essence

which takes its place as life's redemption."

Hmm, how many people think that?

Wallace Stevens was serious about poetry.

Who said, "The whole race

is a poet that writes down

the eccentric propositions of its fate."

Gandhi gets about the same amount of time as Stevens

(as they did in their lives too—Gandhi 79 years, Stevens 76).

A minute or so on Gandhi, not much,

but enough that we are reminded of him,

and think about him, and his statement,

"An eye for an eye leaves the whole world blind" —

while Nat Turner is still fresh in our minds.

INCIDENT AT 69

I am fine with being 69. 70 sounds a little old,

but 69, not so much. It may not be my favorite age,

but it is my favorite number.

It's the year I graduated from college, the Class of '69.

And I got married—same year, same month.

I don't think I realized how huge it all was at the time.

I was sort of floating along.

69 has a nice flow to it, it resembles the yin-yang circle.

And of course there's the wonderful love-making position.

In any case, it's how old I am now, 69.

Last week I was coming out of the supermarket

with my groceries in my re-usable environmentally friendly bag,

re-used a little too long apparently,

because the handle ripped loose, and the bag fell to the ground,

the groceries half-spilling out.

And as I bent down and started to pick them up, suddenly I was joined

by two beautiful young women. Both had long blonde hair.

They seemed to appear out of nowhere.

And they started gathering things up, and helping me put them

back in the bag, and saying friendly things—

I'm guessing they saw me as some poor old gentleman

in need of aid. I could have handled it!

Reflexes still good. Strong enough to carry bags of groceries—

fairly heavy ones, twenty-five pound bags of cat litter, whatever.

But they were so nice, and so unexpected,

I didn't turn them away. I said, "Oh, you are so kind."

That's what came out of my mouth,

a phrase that does have a certain elderly gentleman tone to it.

When the groceries were back in the bag,

the young women disappeared out into the parking lot

as quickly as they came. They could have been angels,

the way they swooped in, while the apples

were still rolling across the blacktop.

I guess it was one of those random acts of kindness.

Actually, I did feel a little disoriented,

thrown off by being mistaken for an old man.

Now that I think about it, maybe they helped me

because they were attracted by my good looks.

ANONYMOUS SAXOPHONE SOLOS

Listening to old music, listening to music

from a long time ago, I was listening

to Phil Spector's Greatest Hits,

and I was bowled over by how many

great songs he produced. And the songs themselves—

they sure sounded good.

Unfortunately Phil Spector went

off the rails, got in a lot of trouble.

He killed a woman.

He's sitting in prison to this day.

Some of the Hits I knew were his,

some I didn't realize,

though I sure knew the songs, from way back when.

Some from before I was even in high school—

but I was already listening

to rock & roll, and rhythm & blues,

and their various permutations

and variations and explorations.

So driving across a wintry countryside,

swooping up and down hills solitary in my car,

70 years old, I am back

in that music again, and happy to be,

ecstatic, maybe.

And I am noticing especially

the saxophone solos

that were so often, almost always,

a part of those songs.

For example, "Spanish Harlem,"

by Ben E. King, whose voice

was rich, and smooth, and soulful.

No doubt you remember it.

I could just as easily have died

without ever hearing it again,

but here it is, filling the car,

and in the middle of it, a lovely saxophone solo,

with strings just before, and just after.

Who was that saxophone player?

I could probably find out,

do a little research, but no,

I'll just leave it at hearing that song,

and thinking how beautifully

the saxophone solo fits in there,

in the middle of that beautiful song.

Now here comes

"Da Do Ron Ron,"

by The Crystals,

and it seems to me, listening to it,

that it doesn't get any better than this.

"Make a joyful noise unto the Lord."

Well, there it is.

"Da Do Ron Ron."

pumping and clattering along.

Thank you, Phil Spector.

Thank you, Crystals.

And thank you musicians

who were in the studio that day,

drums and tambourines, and all the rest,

and especially the saxophone player

who played a short, bopping solo

right in the middle of it,

and then The Crystals came in again

and took the song home to the end

of its perfect two minutes, twenty-six seconds.

It's not just the stars,

who get their names on the label,

or at least the name

of the group they're in,

who make a civilization.

Almost as important, or just as important

in a different, more obscure way,

are the contributions of the others, in the background,

in their glorious moments,

their anonymous saxophone solos.

DO WAH DIDDY DIDDY

At the concert the band, excellent local musicians,

played somewhere in the middle,

"Do Wah Diddy Diddy,"

which may not be the greatest song

ever written, or even of that era,

but it was and is a pretty great song,

both musically and lyrically, if you ask me.

I know it primarily of course

(as you probably do too)

from Manfred Mann's immortal hit,

though it was first recorded by The Exciters,

and there was another version by Reparata and the Delrons.

I remember walking

down the woods road

singing it with Heather.

Do we get less do wah diddy as time goes on?

Maybe, except for the deeper do wah diddy

that comes with age.

I was singing along inwardly as the band

and the lead singer put it out there on the air,

as great a song as I remembered it—

as great a song as "Da Doo Ron Ron,"

or "Rama Lama Ding Dong,"

or for that matter "Papa Oom Mow Mow."

All good songs to know

as time goes on, to sing to yourself.

Just the phrases themselves are good to know.

If someone asks me a question

I can't or don't want to answer,

I sometimes say, not aggressively, but calmly,

Do wah diddy diddy.

It explains, not everything, but a lot, enough.

Do wah diddy diddy dum diddy do.

A CAMPING TRIP IS LIKE A SHOOTING STAR

Slaloming Route 28

in the Adirondack Park

in the canoe-carrying car

solitary after separating

from daughter and grandsons

at Blue Mountain Lake

where they went south

and I went west

after camping four days

on Little Tupper Lake—

little only because

smaller than Tupper,

Little Tupper five miles long,

not a little lake at all,

and known for its winds.

We paddled in

to campsite 3, on its own island.

That was something,

having your own island,

how often does that happen in life?

I'd camped there before, hoped it would be open,

and there it was, no canoe pulled up,

no one there, a vacancy among the trees.

Spacious enough, fire pit, good spot for tent.

Other amenities: Good branch for bear rope —

though bear swimming out to the island, not very likely.

Bathroom facilities — box with lid —

a little way off from campsite.

Going there to check it out, a snake in the path.

Not big, not an anaconda;

harmless, not a rattler.

Just a garter, maybe two feet long.

A healthy looking snake, gleaming black,

and a snake in the path

is always unexpected, is always something.

The boys came running,

but before they could catch it

it quickened and slithered

and disappeared into the rocks under the bushes.

And we wondered, what's the snake population

on a small island — and how did they get out here anyway?

Why did they cross a quarter of a mile of water? So many mysteries.

On one end of the island, sheer rocks, fifteen feet high.

To call them cliffs

wouldn't be lying.

Excellent for jumping off

with grandsons, they old enough, 9 and 12,

me just young enough, 69,

to partake in such sport.

Water at the foot plenty deep,

fifteen or twenty feet.

I couldn't touch bottom, or rather, didn't want to—

it was dark and cold down there.

Climb up rocks, pause, look around, consider.

Then, leap, plummet through thin air,

plunge.

Come up, swim over to rocks, climb up,

do it again, sometimes singly, sometimes together.

We have invented a new Olympic event:

synchronized cliff jumping.

Stand lined up on cliff edge, poised—

1…2…3… Jump!

Everyone doing a cannonball!

Jumping off cliffs is something.

And swimming around

in deep cool water beneath them.

Back at campsite, pretty soon,

the first pair of loons,

coming in close to the island, quietly cruising.

One always hopes they will be here.

Wonderful the way they dip under.

Guess where they will come up,

and never be exactly right.

Next day, set out to paddle

to the far end of the lake,

then go up the winding stream,

with occasional beaver dams

to lift the canoe over.

Have lunch at Rock Pond.

There are some nice lunch rocks there.

But the wind was blowing pretty strong

out on the lake that day, coming right at us,

slow progress, hard going —

so instead we stopped on the sandy beaches

along the north shore,

took long walks along them,

seeing what there was to see.

First in the distance, then, gradually, close up.

Ambling along, walking on sand, sometimes sloshing.

Stopping now and then to swim,

whenever we want to.

Walking along long wilderness beaches is something.

Maybe the weather reports predicting rain

kept people home — for whatever reason,

very few people on the lake,

only three or four canoes or kayaks

passed by the whole day.

Never made it to Rock Pond. Maybe next year.

The next day we crossed the lake

and explored the south shore.

And as we paddled, a bald eagle

came in from behind us, coasting low above us.

"Look—a bald eagle!"

It glided in and landed up ahead of us

in a wind-swept pine

that leaned out over the lake.

A high branch, but close to earth

by eagle standards.

We paddled slow and quiet,

soon could see it clearly,

a clear long moment

of eagle, until it decided

it didn't want this much attention,

hunched its shoulders,

leaned forward, as if it would fall off the branch,

but not falling, instead opening

its wings in take-off nonchalant and powerful

and flapped away over the water

toward parts unknown.

It was really something.

Climbing out of the tent in the morning,

seeing on the tip of the island my daughter

doing her yoga, doing sun salutes,

not just a name, the sun actually rising

above the misty lake stretched out in front of her.

Changeable weather in Adirondack lakes.

The way the wind stirs.

The way you see it coming.

We'd stopped on a rocky island,

big enough to grow a few bushes, but just barely.

Too small to have a name on the map.

We checked it out. We walked around it.

Took a swim off the sloping boulder side.

But all the while we could see

a darkened bank of clouds

gathering at the end of the lake.

And then the rain started, first over there,

then coming toward us,

the riled-up surface moving closer.

It took only a couple of minutes

for the stampeding rain to reach us.

At first we thought it was hail, it hit us so hard.

We stood in the downpour.

It was wild--to say it was thrilling

wouldn't be lying.

Standing on treeless rocky island

in bathing suits,

millions of raindrops

tearing up the lake, pounding down on us.

The boys started yelling,

not in fear, but joy,

of something so wet

and pounding happening—

standing out in the teeming rain on a rock in a big lake.

It was something.

Luckily, no lightning.

It rained a couple of other times during our stay.

It rained in the night as we lay

in the tent. It was still raining

in the morning.

We put on ponchos

and put in some time, slow time,

standing around among the dripping trees.

In another way, that was something too.

Days it didn't rain, after supper we paddled

to the beaver bog, half a mile from campsite,

and in the meandering channel

we practiced the lesson

of being quiet.

The boys got it.

Coming around a curve,

dark shapes moving

in the water ahead

before the whap and splash

which is always a dusky something.

What am I forgetting?

Oh, meals—cooked on Coleman stove,

food from small packages poured into boiling water.

Soup, macaroni, never so delicious—

flavored, as they say, with fresh air and hunger.

Some string beans brought from the garden.

Heating up water for tea in plastic cups—

civilized cups of wilderness tea—so relaxing, sitting

on a log, or canvas folding chair, by the fire. For

breakfast, pancakes flipped carefully

by boy with spatula, with 100% pure maple syrup.

When it's dark, before going into tent,

before rustling into sleeping bags,

sitting on rocky shore,

gazing at sky and seeing a shooting star.

A camping trip is like a shooting star.

And then night, four of us in tent.

Playing cards by flashlight.

Then, complete darkness, lying there waiting

for sleep to come.

And the loons

did not let us down.

Out of the night, out of some corner

of the big cornerless lake,

came their looning,

which is something, if anything is something.

The boys hadn't heard it before, but now they have.

Then the silence itself, still lake night,

just a few campsites here and there, canoes pulled up.

The great silence—

that was really something.

"FRIEND, GOOD" —

AND OTHER OBSERVATIONS

That line was spoken by the Frankenstein monster, still played at that point by the great Boris Karloff. It is from a beautiful and profound scene, the brief interlude of calm and welcoming companionship he experienced while he was living with a blind hermit in his forest hut. I hope all blind hermits had such nice huts in those days. The great Boris Karloff? A friend and I were talking about the high art/popular culture distinction. A conundrum, I said. He was sure that there is such a divide. Certainly anyone can name some works that are clearly on one side, and others that are on the other.

He had noticed on my shelf a still from another famous scene from that movie, *The Bride of Frankenstein:* the newly introduced couple—the monster so hopeful, holding her bandage-swathed hand; the bride, newly made, with her electrified hair, strikingly beautiful, confused, getting ready to scream. My friend had expressed admiration, or was it affection, for the film. Nodding at the photo, I asked, high art or low? He didn't hesitate: low. "Well, maybe," I said. "But, was Boris Karloff a great actor?" We left it there. We had other things we wanted to talk about. No need to decide everything. But anyone who watches either of those scenes without being moved must have a hard heart indeed.

We all have our own preferences, log of experience, perspective. There are archetypes, and there are personal archetypes. I don't want to use the word "iconic." It's so overused these days. I have another friend, a Russian Orthodox nun, who is a painter and carver of actual icons, and I am moved by her work, and also by hearing her talk about it. Her comments are brief and simple. The icons have nothing to do with idolatry; they are windows, into the world she calls sacred, spiritual. For me, poems, and the other art forms as well, are icons. The word "sacred" is not one I feel comfortable with. Does it describe something out there, or something inside us? It isn't clear to me. But spiritual, yes. In icons or in poems, sometimes spirit comes pouring through.

As for my own poems, it's something like that—for me writing them at least. Hoping for some glimpse of spirit. Pouring? A rivulet maybe. A creek talking to itself in the mountains.

Then there is the idea of "a temporary stay against confusion," as Robert Frost described the function of poems. It's amazing how many poets refer to that quote. I think both icons and poems are that, do that. My iconographer friend spends her time making one thing, and I spend mine making another, and I feel a kinship, however different our religious beliefs.

Another kinship that I feel, one that probably seems equally unlikely, is with rhythm and blues; with what came before it, blues, gospel music; and what came out of it, soul music, especially the music of a certain era, when I was young—more or less, the 1960s. In his book *Sweet Soul Music*, Peter Guralnick, another white guy who was young at that time, wrote: "It was for a considerable length of time limited almost exclusively to a black audience which had grown up on the uninhibited emotionalism of the church and to a secret but growing legion of young white admirers who picked up on rhythm and blues on the radio and took it as the key to a mystery they were pledged never to reveal." I had no sense of the pledge, but I definitely felt the emotion and the mystery. Guralnick goes on to say: "In gospel music, the progenitor of the style, a singer is often described as 'worrying' the audience, teasing it, working the crowd until it is on the verge of exploding, until strong men faint and women start speaking in tongues [....] In soul music [...] there is this same sense of dramatic structure, even if the message does not always provide the same unambiguous response."

I would love to sing in a gospel choir, but my background is different and my singing voice is not that great. I think my own version of worrying the audience, or worrying the line, takes the form of a certain digressiveness, following the impulse of feeling and the meandering and delays of thought. Much more low-key. As James Brown said, "I feel so good I want to scream." Sometimes I do too, but the scream takes a ruminative form. As for unambiguous release, I would like some of that in poems, but at the same time I recognize that poetry works more by just the opposite: ambiguous release. It would be cool to have readers/listeners passing out or speaking in tongues at the end of a poem, but it's a lot to hope for. A reverberation in the chest and the mind, an echo of thought, someone saying "hmmm," is also cool.

There are quite a few cultural references in these poems, but I would say, don't worry about footnotes. When Wilson Pickett, Solomon Burke, and Percy Sledge are mentioned, it's partly because they are worth knowing, and partly for the deliciousness of their names—one of the sub-groups of words. Rouben Mamoulian. Orestes "Minnie" Minoso. If one recognizes the reference, already knows something about the person, so much the better. If not, the poem gives some basic information. I am not trying to be esoteric. Far from it. Essentially, it's a form of calling the roll. It's about color and texture. And in general, the drift is praise.

There are also references to places. Local. Specific. There's a walk down the main street of Auburn, New York, running through these poems. A rust-belt city, formerly a population of 30,000, now a couple thousand fewer. Home of William Seward, Lincoln's Secretary of State, and Harriet Tubman. Other places are out in the county, and others a little farther out, in the Adirondacks and the wilds of northern Pennsylvania. An occasional trip to New York City, Philadelphia, or Baltimore. That's the extent of the orbit—a hundred miles or so from my house. Local, like William Carlos Williams, my first poet, wandering around Paterson and Rutherford, describing church bells or the crowd at a baseball game, bowing and smiling when he sees a young woman taking out the trash. Local, like Walt Whitman wandering around Manhattan, crossing Brooklyn Ferry; later, hanging out in rural south Jersey, writing casual descriptions of weeds and insect cries, which would be collected in *Specimen Days*, "the most wayward, spontaneous, fragmentary book ever printed." Wondering if it was too fragmentary, he decided to go ahead with it and "let the melange's lackings and wants of connection take care of themselves."

Sometimes after a reading people have said, "They're sort of like short stories." OK. As my late friend David Budbill said, after many years of writing exquisite poems of narrative and character, a little tired of hearing that comment, "What's wrong with short stories?" Sometimes someone says, "I can't tell where the poem begins and your talking about it ends." That bothers me, since poetry should be elevated speech, right?— but on the other hand, I have worked a long time to try to create a conversational style. I call these compositions poems partly because of the amount of time I spend trying to get the rhythms right. Also for the rhymes, true or slant. I'm pleased when I get something like spontaneity/ homily, multiplication/napkin, or cane/heaven.

As important to me as any poet is Emily Dickinson. So extravagant. So idiosyncratic. Such penetrating, strange and accurate, phrases. "I'm Nobody— Who are you?" She is the great defender, you could say the patron saint, of the introverts of the world. "Tell all the Truth but tell it slant." I'm for that. It's good to have a slant, and to tell it slant. Needless to say, I am not suggesting a competition with Emily Dickinson, who is to poetry what Willie Mays is to baseball. But the style I am dreaming of would be as extravagant and personal as Dickinson, with some slants; but at other times, or at the same time, as direct and accessible as the monster's "Friend, good," though my utterances are a little longer than his. I wonder if that's possible.

Acknowledgments

Some of the poems appeared previously, sometimes in slightly different form, in the following publications:

"Armed Hiker" and "A Camping Trip Is Like a Shooting Star": *The World Engaged: An Anthology of Nature Writing* (Wood Thrush Books).

"The Crows Fly into Town at Dusk": *Birdsong: poems in celebration of birds* (Foothills Publishing).

"Falcon Park": *From the Finger Lakes: A Poetry Anthology* (Cayuga Lake Books).

"Henry Thoreau and Ellen Sewll": *Thoreau Society Bulletin.*

"One of the Ronettes Has Died": *aaduna—an on-line adventure with words and images.*

This book was designed and set in Palatino Linotype by RHWD Industries

Cover art by Melissa Johnson

Photograph of the author by Tess Nelson

Printed by Salem Printing

groundhog
P O E T R Y   P R E S S